ANGELS WITH ANGLES

The Rogue Nuns behind Operation Breakthrough

LORING LEIFER

WordsWorth Books | Kansas City

First Edition 2016

Library of Congress Control Number: 2015920563

ISBN: 978-0-9972508-0-0 Hardback

For permission requests, ordering information, or quantity sales discounts, contact:

WordsWorth Books
3039 Troost
Kansas City, MO 64109
816-329-5259/books@operationbreakthrough.org

Cover and interior design: JR Caines (cainesdesign.com)
Produced by the David Woods Kemper and William T Kemper foundations
Printed in the United States of America by Walsworth

To all who've lent a hand or a heart
to Operation Breakthrough and come
away richer for the experience.

TABLE OF CONTENTS

ACKNOWLEDGMENTS

This book began with Sam Bennett, program manager of the William T. Kemper Foundation, and his counterpart, Kirby Upjohn at the David Woods Kemper Foundation. They recognized the need to capture a great story, and they not only directed funds for it, but they also acted as ambassadors, coaches, editors, and caregivers. They fed and sustained me with wonderful counsel as well as cuisine. Kirby spirited me away monthly for lovely lunches that were both nurturing and inspiring. Their support made creating this book a joyous experience. James Kemper, who is a great and sustaining friend to Sister Berta, Sister Corita, and to Operation Breakthrough, made this book possible by funding it.

The following former and current employees, volunteers, and board members gave me the raw material by sharing their memories: Sylvia Bagby, Anita Bradford, Scott Burnett, Tamara Chaves Cicogna, Carlos Chaves, Connie Crumble, Kim Davis, Sheila Davis, Marilyn Driver, Lesa and Lola Flanagan, Helen Hill, Destiny Hritz, David Kierst, Rich Koch, Sister Theresa Krumps, Angela McFadden, Steve Millin, Harriet Navarre, Mae Richardson, Sister Liz Seaman, Cecelia Sevart, Christine Sill-Rogers, Mary Steeb, Dawn Taylor, Patricia Thompson, Sharon Turner, and Donna Wike. Special thanks to Jennifer Heinemann and Lee Duckett, who not only endured interviews but also spent hours going through the manuscript and tracking down missing pieces. I also benefited from earlier accounts of Operation Breakthrough by Lynley Budimas and Jan Regan.

Three individuals were especially instrumental. Christine Minkler gave me a window into the past through the archive she created. She offered wise advice in approaching my subjects. Claudia York's fine mind and enduring association with the sisters produced numerous keen observations and the only diary from the early days. Susie Roling, a former employee and now close friend of Sr. Berta, shared her deep insights into Sr. Berta and her relationship with Sr. Corita, as well as a treasure trove of funny sayings captured over the years.

The following students recounted adventures and helped me recreate the loving and zany early school days in Chicago and Kansas City: Dwayne Ivory Bradford, Barry Kountz, LaShantese Ward, Stephanie Palmer-Sillimon, John Pellettiere, and Dana Pryor. One former student in particular, Kim Randolph, brought St. Vincent's to life by so generously recounting her memories and impressions. She also shared details of her life beyond the center and helped to give some continuity over the decades.

Others who contributed to the story include Father James Lawbaugh, former pastor of St. Vincent's who recalled the 1960s and '70s with great tenderness. Two people from the Society for Saint Pius X (SSPX), which now occupies the former St. Vincent properties, also gave me a window into the past. Father Jordan Fahnestock, the former school principal, let me explore the church and school at leisure, and Louis Tofari, SSPX historian and writer, provided a marvelous tour and history, as well as resources. Regina Qualls at the Sisters of Charity of the Blessed Virgin Mary motherhouse provided records with real dates. Denise Simeone at the *National Catholic Reporter* helped me understand the Catholic community in the 1970s. Steve Osborne, CPA, whose accounts of the center's most trying times were amazingly detailed—enough to corroborate something I suspected was a myth.

Since most photographs in this book came from shoeboxes, the identities of many photographers and their subjects were long lost. The children's portraits in the last chapters, though, can be credited to Gloria Baker Feinstein. To all the photograhers, named or not, I applaud you for capturing the past.

Writer Deborah Shouse helped with gentle editorial coaching. Audra Spiven, copy editor, added grammatical rigor and accuracy. Mary Esselman, the center's CEO and torchbearer of the sisters' mission, and CFO Cheryl Duffy stepped in as pinch-hitting proofreaders in the ninth inning. Thank goodness for their sharp eyes.

Graphic designer JR Caines added spirit, color, and artistry to every page. I'll be forever awed by how masterfully he designed the pages to augment the story.

Among those likely unaware of their contribution to this book are David Touster, who helped me find the hook and the humor, and my mother, Doreen Leifer, who helped me find the confidence to take on challenges.

My husband, Paul Temme, played a critical role beyond just being a supportive spouse. He gladly came to every Operation Breakthrough event, took a genuine interest in the people as well as the project, and was always willing to discuss editorial challenges. He also helped me see that an imperfect, finished book is better than the possibility of a perfect one never realized. You wouldn't be reading this without him.

Lastly, I am most grateful to Sr. Berta and Sr. Corita, who opened their files, suitcases, and memories to make this happen. They let me read their letters, poke through their possessions, and ask them tough questions. They never attempted to sugarcoat or censor, even when something showed them in an unflattering light. These two women have taken nothing for themselves and have given everything to others—including providing me with two heroines for a story I will always feel blessed to have had the chance to tell.

PREFACE

When Sam Bennett, the program manager of the William T. Kemper Foundation, first called to ask if I was interested in telling the story of the two nuns who started Operation Breakthrough, my first thought was, *This is such a good idea. I can't believe someone hasn't already done it.*

Over the course of the next year, I would discover why. Records were scarce. Most had been either lost, destroyed, or (more likely) not kept in the first place. Sr. Berta and Sr. Corita believe in doing, not analyzing. They spent their time helping others, not thinking about themselves or their motivations, so background explanations were sorely lacking.

What came in abundance, however, were memories. They spilled forth from the sisters, students, staff, parents, board members, and volunteers like seeds from milkweed pods. Facts were sketchy, and details varied widely. There were 400 or 600 children. The loan was to buy a gas station, or no, it was to replace windows. An event happened in 1971, or 1981. It involved thousands more or thousands fewer, or it happened at the hands of different people. I spent more than a year chasing down these seeds, trying to separate fact from fiction.

Thus, what follows is more memoir than history. It weaves together the paltry records, media accounts, extensive conversations with the sisters, and dozens of interviews into a single narrative. (Different typefaces denote when the sisters or someone else is talking.) It attempts to recreate how two nuns conspired with a colorful cast of draft dodgers, hippies, Black Panthers, social activists, and socialites to improve the world, while battling a few bishops and bureaucrats along the way. Time has undoubtedly deformed, embellished, or even rewritten history. I hope this does not trouble my readers, for the stories that live in people's hearts aren't always bound by facts, and truth exists in their spirit.

I did my best to capture the enthusiasm and magic of what these two women created and sustained, but more than once I thought of Gustave Flaubert's definition of language as "a cracked kettle on which we tap out crude rhythms for bears to dance to while we long to make music that will melt the stars." Operation Breakthrough has melted stars, while my mere words will not.

—LL

We are standing on the shoulders of giants.

—Kim Davis, former employee

Srs. Berta Sailer and Corita Bussanmas

CHAPTER 1

NEIGHBORHOOD IN A BOX

Three dozen loaves of just-baked bread waft a warm, yeasty smell in the reception area of Operation Breakthrough. An area baker donates them and, for a brief period each morning, one of the largest childcare centers of its kind in the country smells like home.

For many of the 400 children who come through its doors every day, Operation Breakthrough is the only semblance of a home they have. A majority of them have already suffered traumatic events. They've lost a parent, watched someone killed, suffered or witnessed abuse, or lived without a permanent home.

Operation Breakthrough is a one-square-block respite from their hunger and pain. It provides childcare and education for children from six weeks to 13 years of age. Also onsite is a medical clinic, dentist's office, food pantry, and clothes closet. Social workers, physical and occupational therapists, speech therapists, and psychotherapists also provide services.

At 7:00 a.m., the moms and dads begin dropping off their kids. Shortly after, Sister Berta Sailer, a co-founder of the center, makes the arduous trip up a flight of stairs from her basement office to greet them. At the age of 77, she has trouble with her back and hips. Osteoporosis has etched her bones, and a couple of vertebrae have fractured. She rocks from side to side to move herself forward, but this hardly slows her down. Her eyes shine with wisdom, kindness, and great mischief. It's a formidable combination of resolve and rascality.

Serving as a loving grandmother is the one easy task Sr. Berta will perform today.

She bends down to ask Chuck, a four-year-old foster child, what he wants to be.

"If I grow up, I want to be a fireman," he says.

"Can you imagine that?" she says to the nearby receptionist, after Chuck is out of earshot. "No four-year-old should think that growing up might not be an option. Chuck had to watch his mother's boyfriend kick his two-year-old sister to death."

Another little girl arrives, in soiled clothes. Sr. Berta knows she lives in a home without utilities. She takes the girl by the hand to her office, where she keeps a stash of clean clothing. When they return a few minutes later, the little girl has a gumball, a smile, and a set of clean clothes—including underwear. Her dirty duds go to the onsite laundry.

Sr. Berta knows the names of almost all the kids. She knows who is allergic to peanuts and how many buses one mom takes to drop off her child. She knows who lives in a car and who watched her father push her mother out a second-story window.

Not all live in troubled situations. Three-year-old Kei'Shae, whose parents both work, bounds toward Sr. Berta, excited to begin her day, and, for an instant, the nun forgets all the fires she's fighting and lets the bubbly little girl wrap her in a blanket of joy. After Kei'Shae heads to her classroom, Sr. Berta's shoulders droop with a sense of foreboding about what the week will bring.

She will soon be coming to work alone for the first time in 45 years. Her partner and co-founder of the center, Sister Corita Bussanmus, will retire officially this week in October 2013. At the age of 80, Sr. Corita can be as steely-eyed as ever but now takes longer to find the words she wants. She has a whiskey voice and a rumbling cough from the cigarettes she refuses to relinquish. Heart problems and surgery to unblock her carotid artery have also taken their toll and made working at the center increasingly difficult.

The sisters are deeply devoted to each other. Their relationship is not one of long walks or talks but of shared purpose. They have spent every waking hour working for children and their families, fighting to rebuild neighborhoods destroyed by poverty and urban decay. Their single-minded ministry and more than a few miracles have kept Operation Breakthrough alive for 45 years.

Daycare children at play

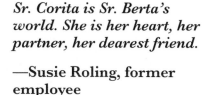

Sr. Corita is Sr. Berta's world. She is her heart, her partner, her dearest friend.

—Susie Roling, former employee

Both sisters have huge hearts and care deeply about the center. The difference between them is that Sr. Berta can't say no, and Sr. Corita can.

—Jenny Horsley, former employee

Sr. Berta at play

> **Sr. Berta's religion is the way she lives her life.**
>
> —Kim Randolph, former student

> **Saying no to Berta is like waving a red cape in front of a bull.**
>
> –Kim Davis, former employee and current head of Amethyst Place

They are both complex figures, full of contradictions. They both took a vow of obedience yet live in defiance of many church conventions. Neither has time to say prayers or spend hours in church, yet they both consider themselves nuns, as does their order. And, while the two sisters are happy to honor their vows to live in poverty themselves, they have spent the bulk of their lives working to help others escape it.

Though they share a mission, the two nuns could not be more different. Tall and stately with a corona of white hair, Sr. Corita views the world as replete with goodness and light, while Sr. Berta, compact and sturdy, is perpetually incensed that she cannot make the world into the beatific place that Sr. Corita sees. Where Sr. Corita stands back, rooted in the confidence of her convictions, Sr. Berta barrels forward, fueled by frustrated energy.

When Sr. Berta rocks the boat, Sr. Corita keeps it afloat. Sr. Berta wonders how she will fare without her friend's tempering influence. She must also carve out a new role for herself. The board appointed a new CEO to oversee the day-to-day management of the center a year ago. Donors, volunteers, and a staff of 130 now make sure the center's kids have toys, a hot lunch, turkey on Thanksgiving, gifts for Christmas, a cake on their birthdays, a pat on the head, or an encouraging word. Hosts of other consistent, caring adults now watch over the children on a daily basis. There is less for Sr. Berta to do.

She wonders what it will be like without Corita. She tries to put this out of mind and return to planning the retirement party, but immediate tasks soon distract her.

GOING IT ALONE

"Where's Dave?" Sr. Berta asks as she marches down the hallway to the center's basement offices. Dave, a volunteer at Operation Breakthrough, is serving a mission requirement by giving a year of service to the center. This week, his Catholic community called him home for a seven-day retreat.

When a staff member tells her this, she harrumphs, "Is this a seven-year retreat? Moses only took 30 days to get the Ten Commandments."

She believes that aiding the poor trumps prayer and reflection. In her mind, the world would be a better place if the devout spent more time helping than clasping hands in prayer. Atop the list of convictions that define her is: *Service trumps religion.*

So anyone who isn't on hand to help in a crisis can expect to take some flak.

As Sr. Berta heads toward her office, employees try to make themselves scarce. One quickly changes direction; another hides behind a manila folder. They fear she may conscript them away from their own work. It doesn't matter if the person is the CEO, the psychiatrist, or a casual visitor; they might find themselves unloading a truck or serving up lunch in a pinch.

New employees quickly discover they can't say no to Sr. Berta, and she has even less respect for job descriptions than she does for rules. The archivist has scrubbed mold from wallboards, the marketing director bought a cage for a hamster, and the grant writer has unloaded trucks. The CEO works for a dollar a year, and that doesn't absolve her from heavy lifting either.

Today, Sr. Berta is looking for help to make sure everything is perfect for Sr. Corita's retirement party. She wants confirmation that the mayor and several council people will attend. She's also trying to find a job for a mom who has just graduated from a medical technology program, and an apartment for another

FUNDING SOURCES

65% - Individual, corporate, and foundation benefactors

35% - Government sources

woman who was living with her two children at a bus shelter near the Power & Light District downtown for a week—and never missed a day of work.

"If only people knew how hard these moms are trying," Sr. Berta says. She has become the go-to person when someone notices a family in trouble. Preachers, politicians, and even the head of United Way call her to report a family living in a car, a young child wandering the streets alone, or a hospital that just discharged a homeless woman and her newborn without even a diaper. They all know Sr. Berta will not stop until she has found a solution.

As age saps her energy, she worries about the future of her families. When Berta speaks about a child, mom, or family member, it is always with possession. They are *her* kids, *her* moms, *her* families, and *her* problems, and she expects those around her to feel the same.

Consequently, her days career like a pinball from one emergency to another. Today is no different. Each phone call and visitor brings a new dilemma. An evicted family needs a place to sleep that night; a childcare worker reports a child who has bruises on her back; a little boy needs a foster home when his mom goes to jail; a mother who lost her son to gun violence needs consoling. Other problems are more prosaic. A parent whose car broke down needs a ride to work; a student needs a bus pass; a mom needs help with a utility bill.

While Sr. Corita has faith in God's beneficence, Sr. Berta's faith is in the corporeal. Her first response to problems is to start calling contacts in her smartphone. Among the 1,800 entries are lawyers, social workers, funders, volunteers, politicians, and football players.

"I have a mom…" is how most of her conversations start. Sr. Berta dials through the list with the single-minded determination of General Sherman through the South until she finds one who is willing and able to

Sr. Corita is the brain, and Sr. Berta is the heart of Operation Breakthrough.

—Cecelia Sevart, former employee

solve the crisis at hand. Many have sworn not to accept her calls anymore, but few make good on those threats.

Steve Millin, an attorney known here as Saint Steve, agrees to help with the eviction case after he learns enough details to suspect that the landlord has violated the law. Susie Roling, a clinical case manager, reports the suspected abuse and agrees to take the soon-to-be-motherless boy. Christine Minkler, Sr. Berta's assistant, gives the stranded parent a ride to work. Sr. Berta hands out money for both a bus pass and a utility bill from her own pocket and tries to comfort the grieving mom.

The sisters do not give up on people, nor do they judge them. "You can send them a mother who is a prostitute who needs childcare, and, as long as she's taking good care of her children, they won't be judgmental about how she makes a living," said David Kierst, a retired juvenile court judge.

Several calls bring cheer. A volunteer calls to report that *The Kansas City Star* will run a feature story on Starfish, the church-based mentoring program that Berta inspired. Scott Burnett, a Jackson County legislator from the 1st District, calls offering to drive his truck to pick up donated furniture. After thanking him, Sr. Berta asks, "What are you doing about all these homeless people?"

Sr. Berta has a well-earned reputation for irreverence, which is on display today. At a meeting to discuss an impending visit from a Missouri legislator, she asks if anyone knows his religion. "If he were Catholic, I could nun him to death. I'll God-bless him all afternoon."

Then, instead, she charms him with a running patter worthy of Groucho Marx on injustices among the poor. She knows that his vote on an upcoming state aid issue could make a difference for the center's families. She first takes him to a roomful of preschoolers and begins:

More than 98 percent of our kids live below the federal poverty line, most far below. The average household income of our families is $9,400 a year. Almost a fourth are homeless or near homeless. They live in cars, run-down hotels, or hop from couch to couch. Many have suffered abuse, neglect, or family crises. There are shelters for homeless pets, but there aren't places for children. If we gave every homeless child a puppy, we would find homes for them. Our pets do so well because everyone has loved a pet. But how many have loved a poor person? Our children should do at least as well as, maybe better than, our dogs. Did you know that the first case of child abuse was prosecuted under animal cruelty laws?

He shakes his head, and she leads him to an area full of toddlers. "The kid who might find a cure for cancer someday could be in this room. So we better make sure he or she gets a good education." Before she's through, she'll make more leaps in topics than Rudolph Nureyev did in ballet shoes. Sr. Berta says:

In the two weeks following the E. coli scare in fresh spinach this year, we had 2,000 cans of spinach donated to the center. What makes people open cabinets and say, "This could kill my kids, but I'll give it to the poor"? These are good people. We've got to get to where there isn't a them and an us. Until people meet each other, that attitude will persist.

Her phone rings, and she fishes her smartphone out of her bra. Kim Randolph, a graduate of the neighborhood school that Srs. Berta and Corita ran almost 40 years ago, still calls every few months. During her childhood, Kim's father was in the military, stationed halfway around the world, and her mother worked two jobs. In the fifth grade, she needed somewhere to go from 6:00 a.m. to 6:00 p.m. every day. St. Vincent's gave her a community.

OPERATION BREAKTHROUGH BY THE NUMBERS (2015)

96 Children in infant-toddler program (up to 2 years)

170 Children ages 2-5 in daycare

98 Children ages 6-13 in before/after school programs

110 Children ages 6-13 in full summer program

87 Percent of families who live in poverty (below $12,898 a year)

21 Percent homeless at some point during the year

81 Percent who rely on food stamps or other benefits to survive

83 Percent African American or mixed race

14 Percent white

2 Percent Hispanic

1 Percent other

119 Full-time employees (22 part-time)

450 Volunteers

$7.4M Operating budget in 2015

Sr. Berta stuffs the phone back into her bra and picks right back up with the legislator:

People think our moms are drug addicts who are too lazy to work but energetic enough to have eight kids. A typical parent is a single mom with two or three kids. She works two jobs and gets up early to bring her kids here. She shops at thrift stores, gets food stamps, and can barely survive.

With Operation Breakthrough, she can. But if she gets a 10-cent raise from her minimum-wage jobs, she loses her food stamps and childcare benefits. That's insane.

Standing in front of the center's kitchen that serves 1,000 meals a day, she continues:

You can't educate a kid who's hungry. Do you know that a mass murderer can get food stamps in Missouri, but someone with a drug conviction can't? We have a mom, Molly, who gets food stamps for her kids. Because she's a drug felon, she can't use them to feed herself. A mass murderer could get them for himself. Molly cannot. That's absurd.

People who have walked in the shoes of the homeless should be the only ones who can make or apply laws that affect them. There was a judge who sentenced a homeless woman for felony trespassing because she went into an abandoned house to sleep. That's not a felony. That's someone not having resources. That's stupidity on the judge's part.

The legislator tries to keep up with her commentary, sometimes shaking his head in amazement. They stop to watch a room full of three-year-olds playing with blocks, looking at picture books, and playing dress-up. They giggle and squeal with delight. Sr. Berta tells the legislator their histories:

Do you see that little girl working a puzzle? Her mother was a teenager when she was born. At 19, her mom gave birth to a boy. She got frustrated with the baby and banged his head against a table. That little girl watched as her mother killed her newborn brother.

The little boy over there has asthma. His mom, who works at a nursing home, had to beg her employer to take back a raise. It would have disqualified

her from the Medicaid benefits that pay for his medication. The drugs would cost her a few hundred dollars a month that she can't afford.

The legislator clucks and shakes his head in sympathy. Then Sr. Berta stuns him with a left hook worthy of Joe Frazier:

Earlier this month, you voted to reject a bill that called for taxpayers to subsidize Medicaid in Missouri. Why are you cutting health insurance benefits for 300,000 people in Missouri? You can get health insurance from the state, and the taxpayers subsidize your premiums. Why did you take away help for the people who need it most?

The legislator looks away uncomfortably and tries to explain budget pressures.

Although the topics may change, her battle is constant. She crusades against the injustices that keep the poor from rising. For Sr. Berta, whatever she has to do to right wrongs justifies the means.

"A good fight keeps me alive," Sr. Berta says.

While the tour is under way, a reporter interviews Sr. Corita for a story related to her retirement. He asks her what she considers to be the secret to her success.

"The first thing that comes to mind is my stupidity. I didn't know that people who knew better considered our mission impossible."

ALL MY CHILDREN

Over the years, more than 8,000 children have come through the doors of Operation Breakthrough. They have played games, learned life lessons, eaten hot meals, gone fishing, seen the circus, and listened to a symphony or opera. They have gotten a chance to escape from a childhood where dodging bullets, losing family members, and sleeping in abandoned buildings are mundane.

"Our children have so little consistency in their lives," Sr. Berta says. "They ask each other, 'Where do you stay?' instead of, 'Where do you live?' "

Today, Berta opens her mail to find an envelope from Andre Fulson, a former student serving time in prison. Every month, he sends her five dollars from his prison salary, along with a poem and a letter. This month, he tells her he is starting an organization to encourage other inmates to contribute to Operation Breakthrough. He signs off with: "Because of the unconditional love which you always showed me, I learned to love others and the importance of being a caring friend."

Sr. Berta heads toward Sr. Corita's office to show her the letter.

On the wall across from Corita's desk are rows of pictures of the foster children she and Sr. Berta have taken care of over the past 20 years. Piles of papers almost obscure Sr. Corita behind her desk. A couple of mismatched chairs, a small round table, file cabinets, a computer, a fax machine, an old console TV, and bags and boxes of donated toys, clothes, books, stacks of diapers, and a few bicycles further clutter the space. Small screens allow her to monitor the front desk, the back door, and the playground.

Sr. Corita looks at the monitor that shows children playing and tries to remember Andre as a young boy. "He is a beautiful soul." She sighs, and then she turns her radiance to a pile of boxes.

"Can you believe this?" she asks Sr. Berta. "A member of a sewing circle left boxes of quilts to cover inner-city beds. Isn't it amazing the generosity of people?"

Sr. Berta shakes her head, in awe of her friend's attitude and in doubt of her convictions.

They talk about plans for the party, and Sr. Berta leaves, alluding to surprise visitors who may attend.

Shortly after, Mayor Sylvester "Sly" James calls to tell Sr. Berta he will attend the party.

WOW, WHAT A RIDE

Sr. Berta's office is equally cluttered but in a more orderly, artful way—with more sketches, drawings, and quotes. They reflect the diversity of sources from which she draws inspiration, such as:

"It is easier to build strong children than it is to repair broken men." —Frederick Douglass

"Be the kind of woman that when your feet hit the floor each morning, the devil says, 'Oh crap, she's up.' " —Unattributed

A wall plaque quotes Ernesto "Che" Guevara, the Marxist revolutionary from Argentina: "If you tremble with indignation at every injustice then you are a comrade of mine."

Not far from a drawing of Mother Teresa is a Hunter Thompson quote: "Life should not be a journey to the grave with the intention of arriving safely in a pretty and well-preserved body, but rather to skid in broadside in a cloud of smoke, thoroughly used up, totally worn out, and loudly proclaiming, 'Wow! What a Ride!' "

And what a ride it has been for the two sisters brought together by a fire.

Operation Breakthrough, 3039 Troost, Kansas City

Sr. Mary Otto (Corita)

Sr. Berta

CHAPTER 2

ANGELS ON FIRE

When Sr. Berta Sailer first walked into the class of fifth graders in December 1958 in the temporary classrooms for the Our Lady of the Angels Catholic school in Chicago, the 22-year-old nun had no idea what to expect. She felt overwhelmed and unprepared to face the 60 children whose grief was still raw.

She had completed her practice teaching at St. Vincent de Paul Elementary School at 651 W. Lake Street in Chicago and stayed on after graduation to teach kindergarten. She was still in her first year when she got an emergency call from her order, Sisters of Charity of the Blessed Virgin Mary (BVM), to report to Our Lady of the Angels (OLA).

A fire had ripped through the school, killing 92 children and three nuns. While the ashes still smoldered, church officials had to arrange almost overnight to bus the survivors to other schools. Nearby parochial schools took about 400 children. The remaining 1,200 went to three public elementary schools: Rezin Orr, Daniel R. Cameron, and John Hay.

The church sent Sr. Berta to John Hay. A few feet outside her classroom, she could hear whimpering. Compact and athletic, she moved with swift grace into the classroom.

On the same floor in a nearby classroom, Sr. Otto faced a class of second graders. In 1955, after the young woman born Corita Bussanmas took her final vows and new name, the BVM order sent her to teach at Annunciation Elementary School on Chicago's Near North Side. The parish was in a stable, suburban neighborhood with many Irish and Polish families. Sr. Otto quickly fell in love with the children and their families, although her quiet, steady demeanor didn't always make her affection apparent to her students. She was a strict disciplinarian who wasn't above throwing a dictionary at a misbehaving student.

Three years later, at 25, she stood tall and imposing, like a lighthouse with a searching gaze. She recited a prayer for strength as the children filed like young war refugees into the classroom. She thought of the prayer the BVM nuns recited every day for protection from fire as she marched into her new classroom.

The prayer arose after a fire in 1849 destroyed the BVM motherhouse, convent, school, and chapel in Dubuque, Iowa. It protected the school's staff with BVM sisters until Monday, December 1, 1958.

THE LAST NORMAL DAY

The children who attended kindergarten to eighth grade at Our Lady of the Angels School in Chicago had just returned from the Thanksgiving holiday. The day was nearing its conclusion without event. Around 2:20 p.m., teachers started assigning students in each class the task of emptying the day's wastebaskets into large, metal bins in the boiler room.

Only steps away, some refuse burning in a cardboard trash drum went unnoticed. The heat caused a basement window to burst, which supplied oxygen to fan the flames. A fire door protected the classrooms on the first floor from the smoke, but the second floor didn't have one. Soon, fire and smoke engulfed the second floor hallway of the north wing.

Smoke began to roll into classrooms like massive bales of gray cotton, often followed by explosions as fire burst through glass transoms above the doors. The heat and acrid smoke chased the children to the windows, where they screamed for help. Some jumped, but many couldn't reach the windowsills that were 37 ½ inches from the floor.

One father who lived nearby smelled smoke and rushed to the scene. He saw his son in a crowd of young faces frantically pushing to jump out of a second-floor window. He yelled to his son not to jump and went to get a ladder from his garage. When he set it under the window, he found it was too short. "Jump!" he screamed to his son, who was in the fourth grade. Just as his son managed to reach the high windowsill, flames pulled him back inside the classroom, and the father watched in impotent desperation as the fire swallowed his son.

A fire destroyed Our Lady of the Angels school on December 1, 1958

I had 60 children in my classroom in the morning and another 60 in the afternoon and was all by myself. Those were the days, when teachers said, 'Sit down,' and the kids did.

—Sr. Berta

The Chicago Fire Department didn't receive a call about the fire until 2:42 p.m., more than 20 minutes after it started. The panicked caller gave the address of the rectory at 3808 West Iowa Avenue instead of the school, which was at 909 North Avers Avenue, around the corner and half a block away. When the firemen realized the error, a locked gate in front of a courtyard further delayed them from reaching the children who screamed from the classroom windows.

To Sleep with the Angels: The Story of a Fire, by David Cowan and John Kuenster, describes the scene that greeted the firefighters:

Black smoke was billowing from every open space on the building's upper story. Horrified parents were running back and forth screaming as children at the windows were throwing out objects, hanging off the sills, dropping or hurtling themselves to the ground. Scores of inert bodies—children who had already jumped or had been pushed out the windows by classmates— covered the pavement…

The fire had been burning for nearly 30 minutes before help arrived. The delay in reporting, wrong address, and locked gate were only a few of the cruel twists of fate that allowed the fire to destroy so many lives.

School policies also cut off escape. Only the school's principal could ring the fire alarm, but Mary St. Florence Casey was substituting for a sick teacher and was not in her office.

Sister Therese didn't want to violate the strict rule about not leaving the building before the fire alarm went off. "We can't go until we are told. Let's pray," she told her students.

One fourth grader said his teacher, Sister Seraphica, instructed the class, "Everyone say a Hail Mary, and when the firemen come, we can leave."

When heat shattered the transom window, and smoke poured into Sister Geraldita's classroom, she tried to lead her class in the Rosary before she finally

corralled the children and started pushing them out of the window.

Other nuns behaved heroically, crawling along the floor to lead their charges to safety and going back into the building to make sure they didn't leave any children behind. One of the priests, Father Joseph Ognibene, braved the fire to rescue dozens of children by hoisting them to safety. Father Charles Hund managed to get a locked fire door open and evacuate the only classroom on the second floor in the north wing that did not have a single fatality.

Lieutenant Charles Kamin from Hook and Ladder 35 balanced atop a ladder and hoisted children out by their belts so quickly that he didn't have time to make sure they landed on the ladder. He figured a broken leg would be preferable to death by fire.

To Sleep with the Angels recounts as the firefighters went through the school after quelling the blaze:

Guided by lanterns and flashlights, the men groped their way forward through the smoke, searching for life. What they found instead was a gruesome scene of death that would forever be etched in their memories. The devil himself could not have created a more horrible picture.

Strewn about the smoky, blackened classrooms, amid the charred woodwork and caved-in ceilings, were piles of small bodies. Overturned desks and charred books and papers bore witness to the swift unexpectedness of the blaze. Water-drenched plaster and wood lathing hung down from what were once the walls…. With tears streaming down their faces, the firemen crawled into the rooms, hacking at the debris to reach the bodies.

At 4:19 p.m., the fire commissioner declared that the worst school fire in United States history was out.

The next day, the pale, moon-like faces of the 87 children and three nuns who died in the fire haunted the front pages of newspapers across the country. About 140 more children lay in hospital beds, suffering from severe burns, shattered bones, and cuts. Five of

The fire was front-page news across the country

these children would succumb to their injuries in the coming months, bringing the total killed to 95.

The ones who didn't survive the fire were taken to the morgue. When desperate parents could not find their children at any of the seven area hospitals that took fire victims, they had to go to the morgue to identify their children. Most of them were burned so badly they were beyond recognition.

ANGER IN THE ASHES

In their first days at Our Lady of the Angels, Srs. Berta and Otto heard accusations and recriminations run through the close parish almost as fast as the flames.

The OLA parish was one of the largest in the Archdiocese of Chicago with 4,500 registered families, mainly Italian and Irish immigrants. The men mainly worked in trades or held city jobs, such as policemen or firemen. The women were homemakers. It was like a close-knit village—until the fire.

Parents of students asked them, *How could this have happened? How did the fire start? Did someone deliberately set the blaze? Why didn't the alarms sound sooner? Why didn't someone summon the fire department sooner? How could the fire burn for so long without attracting attention? Is the church trying to cover up what really happened?*

Why did so many children die?

The two young nuns were unsettled by the answers in the coming days. The school only had one fire escape, and staff kept it locked, blocking a critical path to survival. The fire alarms were too high up on the walls for any child to reach. Like many others of its day, the school didn't have sprinklers or smoke detectors. Municipal codes required new schools to have fire-protection devices, but older, laxer codes governed the existing schools like OLA.

Many of the teachers instructed their students to kneel down and pray. In 1958, nuns weren't accus-

Despite the investigations and the subsequent confessions of two boys to starting the fire, these questions have remained without definitive answers.

The fire spared the nearby church

tomed to taking action on their own. They awaited orders. The Catholic Church restricted their lives to praying, teaching, nursing, and consoling. They went where their orders sent them and depended on a mother superior to dole out bus fare…or pull a fire alarm.

The passivity of the nuns enraged the parents, as well as the two young sisters newly tasked with teaching the grieving survivors. Srs. Berta and Otto whispered that dozens more children might be alive today had the teachers taken some initiative and disobeyed the rules.

The diocese tried to quell questioning and return the parish to routine. The church leaders wanted to get "everything back to normal." Their hope was to distract the parishioners from their grief. They contacted Catholic Charities for nuns to replace the ones who had perished or were too traumatized to teach. The organization contacted the BVM order, which had been supplying teachers to parochial schools in Chicago since 1867. Among those it ordered to the devastated parish were Srs. Berta and Otto.

On the first morning of school after the fire, the two sisters rode the same school bus, crowded with children who were headed to their various substitute classrooms around Chicago. Some of the children whispered in panicked voices. Some stared blankly ahead, while others cried openly.

Sr. Berta put her arm around a sobbing child and was so focused on giving comfort that she didn't notice the other young nun who had climbed aboard.

Both had taken their vows during the 1950s. They were part of a wave of young women flocking to convents. The population of sisters in the United States grew from about 150,000 in 1951 to a peak of 185,000 in 1965. Other than choosing the same order and being born into the same decade, the two young nuns could not have been more different.

A MOTHERLESS CHILD

Berta had a lonely childhood. Her mother disappeared from her life when she was a toddler, leaving her grandmother, who worked full-time, to raise her. Her grandmother, Bertha Seifert, was born on November 23, 1889, in Austria. She came to the United States on September 26, 1913, on the *France*, which sailed from Le Havre. The ship's manifest listed her as a 24-year-old woman traveling alone from Prutz, Tyrol. She was described as a five-foot, four-inch "domestic laborer" with fair hair and blue eyes. She was bound for 740 Blackhawk Street on Chicago's Near North Side.

She may have left a young infant behind because, when she returned from a trip back to Europe in 1922, the ship's manifest showed her traveling with her 10-year-old daughter, Cecelia, who was born in Prutz. Bertha was now a housewife, having married Paul Josef Sailer. They lived at 1972 Devon Avenue in Chicago.

Cecelia quit school at the age of 17 in 1929, the same year her father (Berta's grandfather) died. She went to work at the American Medical Association. On December 10, 1936, Cecelia, then 24, gave birth to a daughter, Judith Felice. Judith, who would eventually change her name to Berta, didn't remember her mother, nor did she have any knowledge of her father. Her baptismal certificate from St. Jerome's Church listed her father as *pater ignotus* (unknown).

The 1940 U.S. census showed a four-year-old girl living at 1340 West Lunt Avenue in Chicago in a boardinghouse with five other residents, including her mother, Cecilia Sailer, and her grandmother, Bertha Sailer. Cecelia left soon after, leaving her young child with her widowed grandmother in the rough, West Side neighborhood.

The first home Berta remembers was at 6921 N. Clark Street, near Rogers Park. Her grandmother worked full-time ironing clothes at a laundry, so Berta spent a lot of time alone.

After classes at St. Jerome's Elementary School, she rode the streetcar to the Farwell Avenue pier in Chicago to go fishing in Lake Michigan. Sometimes her grandmother took her to the beach after working all day. Her grandmother was in her 70s, and Berta sometimes wished she had a young mom who could show her how to put on makeup and do her nails.

When Berta was in the fifth grade, her grandmother went to work as a cook at a convent nearby. She worked long hours, and Berta was on her own.

Berta in high school

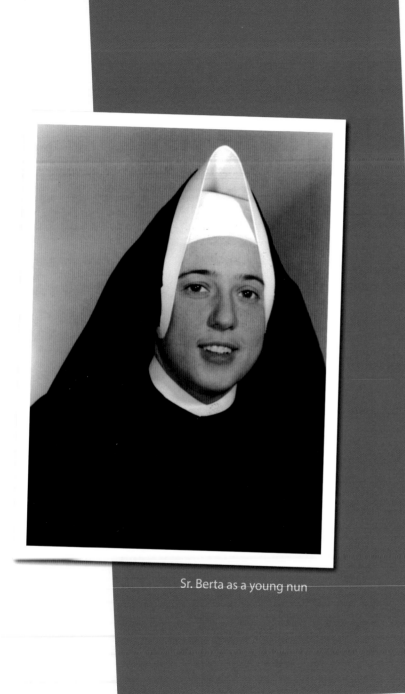

Sr. Berta as a young nun

Now she rode her bike to go fishing alone. She didn't like to leave the pier until she had caught enough fish—mostly perch and crappie—for dinner, even though she knew her grandmother would worry if she didn't make it home before dark. On the way home, she faced the west wind, which slowed her progress, so she put her head down and pedaled harder. Berta was sturdy and compact with a natural athleticism. Sr. Berta says:

I played volleyball, basketball, and baseball. I was also a lifeguard for a while. I became a Girl Scout and went to a scout camp every summer in Illinois. There was a horse stable in Chicago. Around the eighth grade, I started riding my bike to the stable, where you could rent horses. I'd help feed the horses and clean up the stalls in exchange for an occasional ride.

I wanted a horse for my graduation. Needless to say, I didn't get one.

I went to Immaculata High School, an all-girls high school. By then, my grandma worked as a cook there. I came in the evening to help with the dishes. Nuns didn't used to have to do their own cooking or dishes. I got paid five dollars a week.

Money was tight for Berta and her grandmother, but it was worse for many around them. Families in the neighborhood were struggling, and Berta felt the impulse to help. As her graduation approached, she thought about what to do next. She saw her options as limited to staying home, raising kids, or becoming a teacher.

"If I wanted to do anything, being a nun was an avenue," she said. She dreamed of going to Africa as a medical missionary with the Maryknoll Sisters, but this would have left her grandmother alone.

After graduating high school in June 1954, she applied to the BVM convent at Mount Carmel in Dubuque, Iowa. The admission form asked, *Are you of legitimate birth?* She left the line blank. The reason she stated on the form for wanting to become a sister was almost as inscrutable. "I want to dedicate my life to God as a Sister of Charity of the Blessed Virgin Mary."

Education was an important component of the BVM order. The order began in 1833, when four women from Dublin came to Philadelphia to teach the city's poorest children and consecrated themselves as an order. In 1845, they moved to Dubuque, Iowa, where BVM nuns established a boarding school there that later became Clarke University.

The bucolic campus that bordered the Mississippi River appealed to Berta's love of nature. The 100-acre grounds afforded walking trails, dense woods, and striking river vistas.

BVM motherhouse in Dubuque, Iowa

Its religious appeal to Berta was less apparent.

Perhaps having the attentions of a mother superior and other young nuns filled a maternal need. She had grown up without a mother, siblings, or much family life. Convent life would surround her with a loving, caring community. The order would provide the family she didn't have.

At Mount Carmel, Berta went from being a postulate (a woman who has stated her intentions to be a nun) to a novice (an official candidate the religious order has deemed suitable for sisterhood). She chafed at the rules and regimented life and was frequently at odds with her superiors. Sr. Berta admits:

I wasn't crazy about it. The sisters came close to throwing me out for breaking rules. I was eager to become a novice, which would involve going back to Chicago to study.

The BVM order sent me to Mundelein College, which the order founded in 1931. I lived in a scholasticate, a building for young nuns that was 10 blocks from my grandmother's house. I got a BA degree with a major in education and history. For about a year during this time, I went to the Art Institute of Chicago. I did mostly design work, creating posters, banners, and collages. I wasn't skilled at drawing or painting. A teacher asked us to draw a picture of someone holding a baby. The head of the baby I drew was bigger than body of the person holding it.

She was officially received into the order in March 1955 and took her first vows two years later. She wanted to take the name Sister Bertha to honor her grandmother, but it was taken, so she became Sister Mary Berta. She promised to forswear worldly goods, marriage, and sexual intercourse and do the bidding of her superiors.

According to *Double Crossed: Uncovering the Catholic Church's Betrayal of American Nuns*, by Kenneth Briggs, "…nuns were to resist worldliness and to aspire to a spiritual ideal that required a degree of discipline that was more restrictive and exacting than that expected of anyone else in the Catholic religion. Theirs was a 'state of perfection' whose daily customs included virtually nothing that the sisters chose freely for themselves."

Sr. Berta was only 22 years old and still in her first year as a teacher in Chicago when she got the call on December 2, 1958, to report to Our Lady of the Angels.

Across town was another nun who grew up under much different circumstances.

SIBLINGS GALORE

Born in 1933, Corita Noel Bussanmas was the second from the youngest child in a close family of eight children. The family lived in a middle-class neighborhood in Des Moines, Iowa. Her father, Otto Bussanmas, was a mechanic, and her mother, Mary, worked for the Internal Revenue Service. Her parents were

I don't know why I became a nun. I still wonder to this day. I was 18 years old—as if an 18-year-old knows what she wants to do.

—Sr. Berta

Sr. Berta lives on the edge of Catholic. She will break any rule and do whatever it takes.

—Mary Steeb, a longtime supporter

My mother was like Berta. When she told you to do something, you did it NOW.

—Sr. Corita

It wasn't until the 1960s that the church allowed nuns to keep their birth-given names.

Corita at first communuion

practicing Catholics; they stressed the importance of service to the community. The children heeded these admonitions. Corita's oldest sister became a nun. Two other sisters became nurses; one brother joined the Army and the other the Navy. She describes her childhood:

We were part of a neighborhood with lots of children of all races. We never thought about what color we were. We all played together…baseball, basketball, and football. I was a calm child and didn't like to fight. I wanted peace at all costs. I took after my father. He was a meek, mild man. My mother was the excitable one. She was a real stickler. If she said jump, he would. He would do anything for her. I felt sorry for him.

I used to spend holidays with my sister when she was at St. James in Washington, Iowa. Because my sister was 18 years older than I was, it was a rare occasion when we were all together. She had already entered the convent when I was born.

St. James was a nice, small convent, very homey. The nuns didn't walk around with their hands folded and their heads bowed like you saw in the movies. They had a lot of fun. They laughed, played games, and listened to music.

I went to a Catholic boarding high school, Immaculate Conception Academy, in Davenport, Iowa. I was happy there; the nuns pushed us to have fun. We'd go to dances and roller skate. The boarders from Chicago introduced us to smoking and drinking. We thought we were wild. I was never a troublemaker, though.

After graduating from Immaculate Conception on May 30, 1952, Corita went to Mount Carmel Convent in Dubuque. On her application for admission, she stated, "I want to be a sister because that is what I think God wants me to do. I have had the inclination all through high school." (Her rationale had a certainty and clarity that Sr. Berta's lacked.)

When the order officially received Sr. Corita in March 1953, she took the name Sister Otto to honor her father. Her last year at the convent coincided with Sr. Berta's first year there, although their paths didn't cross.

Where Sr. Berta railed against the rules of convent life, Sr. Otto thrived under them. She made friends with her fellow sisters. They strolled around the grounds and breathed in the traditions that emanated from the 100-year-old buildings. She felt serene there.

Corita (center) with her brother James and sister Janet

Five years later, the BVM motherhouse ordered her to leave her teaching post and report to Our Lady of the Angels. Both sisters showed up just a few days after the fire with the leather steamer trunks that carried all of their worldly goods.

TWO CONSOLING NOVICES

The two nuns had their first encounter at the OLA convent, a three-story building made of bricks the color of dried blood. The convent housed about three dozen nuns. Most of them were decades older than Srs. Berta and Otto, so the two young nuns gravitated toward each other. They began their friendship by talking about how their students were faring in the first days after the fire.

Although they were both trained teachers, they had little experience dealing with the grief and psychological trauma the fire caused.

In *To Sleep with the Angels*, David Cowan and John Kuenster describe the first day of school after the fire on Tuesday, December 9, 1958:

The children were assembling by classroom. In one class there were just three kids left who weren't dead, burned, or seriously injured. So it was very traumatic for those kids. It was a bitter cold day. When the kids came back at four o'clock in the afternoon that first day, the parents were all there to meet them. They were still terrified. They didn't want to let those kids out of their sight.

The children were uneasy as well…. Some youngsters were frightened by the thought of climbing stairs and sitting in classrooms two and three stories up.

One day at John Hay, the heating system emitted some fumes from cleaning fluid, and the children in Sr. Berta's class ran out of the building, sure that this school would also burn down. She ran out after them to assure them that there was no fire.

Corita with her parents,
Otto and Mary Bussanmas

Fire victim Billy Edington

The priests, the OLA school principal, and most of the older nuns were made of sterner stuff. They all stressed getting back to routine and not dwelling on the tragedy. Most of the nuns discouraged the kids from ever talking about the fire. Srs. Berta and Otto questioned whether this was the right thing to do. Their instincts were to comfort and coddle, not enforce routines. It wasn't long before this would test their vows of obedience. Sr. Berta says:

The parish had no idea what to expect from the grieving congregation, so it arranged for a policeman to protect the convent. There were a lot of angry parents who had made threats against the nuns they believed were responsible for the deaths of their children. There were people who wanted to kill the pastor too. The policeman was in the convent for several months. There were policemen in the classrooms as well.

We were all on edge, especially the children who lived through the fire.

Someone in Sister Andrea's classroom yelled, "Fire!" one day. A little boy rushed to the window, took a rope out of his book bag, and proceeded to crawl out the window. Sister Andrea socked him and knocked him out cold to keep him from jumping. Some of the nuns had a rougher approach to counseling and were more conservative than Otto and I were.

At lunchtime, we went to St. Anne's Hospital to visit the young burn victims. A little boy name Billy Edington was burned over 70 percent of his body. He was locked into a device that turned him over to keep his burned flesh from sticking to the bed linens. He underwent 25 skin graft surgeries before he passed away.

A month after the fire, the pope sent papal blessings to each of the parents who lost a child. We had to deliver them to their homes. This was a neighborhood of old-country Italians and Irish. In most homes, there was a shrine to the lost child with pictures and trinkets.

Not all the nuns in the OLA convent could deal with the situations. According to Sr. Berta, two wound up in mental hospitals. The two young nuns struggled to console the families, but grief sometimes overwhelmed them. They were also deeply troubled by accounts of those who survived the fire. They learned that several nuns had instructed the children to pray while they awaited the school principal's order to evacuate the building, per school policy. Taking action would have likely saved many lives.

Monument to fire victims at Our Lady Queen of Heaven Cemetery in Chicago

Sr. Berta vowed to her new friend that she would never follow a rule that might put a child in harm's way, and she would do whatever it took—legal or otherwise—to keep children safe.

Sr. Otto pointed out that this vow might be at odds with the ones they took as nuns. Circumstances would soon make this disparity clear to both of them.

Srs. Corita and Berta in Chicago

CHAPTER 3

THE WEST SIDE JOKERS

The nuns in the OLA convent were abuzz. Three years after the fire, a new kind of crisis faced the parish—neighborhood gangs.

Yesterday, some of the rowdy neighborhood boys beat up Father Frank Cantieri with a two-by-four board. At six feet, four inches tall, he was one of the church's most imposing pastors. He had started a teen club in an OLA-owned building on Hamlin Avenue known as The Hall. After this incident, he shut down the club.

Teenagers were getting into more serious trouble. Gang fights were common in the area. The Humboldt Park neighborhood was a much grittier place than it had been a decade ago. Many of the middle-class Irish and Italian families found it too painful to stay in the area after the fire. According to the Our Lady of the Angels website:

The fire had a devastating impact on the surrounding community. Many of the families and friends of the victims moved away because they could not remain near reminders of the fire. Fire related exodus paired with the nationwide urban population shifts of the 1960s led to rapidly changing neighborhood demographics.

Small factories were closing, jobs disappearing. Two big plants in the area, Helene Curtis Cosmetics and Schwinn Bicycles, also closed. Emigrants from Puerto Rico and Mexico replaced those from Europe.

The parish was changing as well. All signs of the original school were gone. The diocese had razed the remains of the school building only two months after the fire. Construction on a new building began in June 1959.

Cardinal Meyer dedicated the newly rebuilt OLA school on October 2, 1960. The three-story, concrete-reinforced structure had a sprinkler system and smoke detectors connected to the precinct's main office. Public donations from around the world paid for most of the $1.25 million structure.

Determined not to reference the fire directly, the cardinal's homily at the dedication included the words: "Trust God, and he will help… It is his example which gives courage to continue to believe in divine providence, despite appearances to the contrary, because of suffering, sin, or disaster. Here in this school of Our Lady of the Angels, we understand better the meaning of our Lord's word: 'Suffer the little ones to come unto me…for such is the kingdom of heaven.' "

THE SISTERS, THEY ARE A-CHANGIN'

Getting through the days and months following the fire had begun to change Srs. Berta and Otto, as well as the neighborhood. They gained insight into the children of the parish and the neighborhood. Within a few years, Mother Superior Sister Mary Rose Esther moved Sr. Otto from teaching second graders to sixth graders, a much more challenging post.

Sr. Berta became known as Sister Wirer, not only for her prowess with audio-visual equipment but also for her ability to "unscramble and recast" fifth graders. A profile of her by Catherine A. Daly in the parish newsletter said that she "assembles persons, places, and things into a working collective…. Her complete dedication to her profession heartens us all, and OLA is a better place because this gifted, versatile, and unselfish little nun is in our midst."

Both sisters gained confidence and ambition. Together, they started a Spanish Club and put on shows with their students.

Sr. Otto asked Sr. Mary Rose Esther for permission to return to college to get her bachelor's degree. Most nuns teaching in parochial schools had neither teaching certificates nor degrees. Sr. Otto wanted to know more about how children learn and develop. She started attending classes during the summer at the BVM-run Clarke College in Dubuque. Sr. Berta stayed in Chicago.

The separation fueled tender letters back and forth. Sr. Otto wrote one on the back of a school map, reporting on her classes and relating that

The Our Lady of the Angels school that replaced the one destroyed by fire

Loretto Heights College
Office of the Registrar

Report of

SISTER MARY OTTO BUSSANMAS

☐ Mid-Semester ending

☐ For Semester ending

Courses	Grade	Sem. Hrs.
SS – 1965		
Ed., 313– Guidance and Mental Hygiene	B	3

Sister Mary Christopher
Registrar

Report card from a summer school class Sr. Corita took

she had typed two papers for a fellow sister. She also expressed gratitude for her light duty, which was "filling the sugar bowls every other day." She counseled Sr. Berta about taking her vitamin pills and trying to be patient. She signed off with, "Be good and let time take its course. Patience is a virtue; so is trust. You are truly great. Love and prayers, Sr. Otto, BVM."

After Sr. Berta visited her in Dubuque, Sr. Otto thanked her, saying, "Sr. Berta, you really edify me to the nth degree."

They had become friends who trusted each other. Although the Catholic Church admonished against nuns forming "particular friendships" (i.e., showing an interest in one sister over another), the devotion, tenderness, and understanding these two young nuns had for each other sang in their letters.

Worries always seemed to chatter incessantly in Sr. Berta's mind like a murder of crows, and she began to confide her anxieties to Sr. Otto, who responded:

Dear Sister,

You dear "Berta buddy" have made me very <u>human</u> and dearie <u>never</u> have I ever been so lonesome. Feelings are too real, aren't they? This separation is good for both of us I'm sure, but it certainly hurts in this purifying process… God has been good to me to let me have such a good friend!

God does work in strange ways and much good has come and will come from your minute by minute acceptance of your cross.

No dear, you are not a poor Simon of Cyrene. He could actually see his cross coming to an end… You dear, have none of this physical consolation.

…Dearie, since you have had no relief from the excruciating tortures at night, I think it is only fitting for me to do physical penance to try if possible to win you relief. It has been no problem at all giving up candy, therefore, not much sacrifice. Beginning tonight, I will not eat

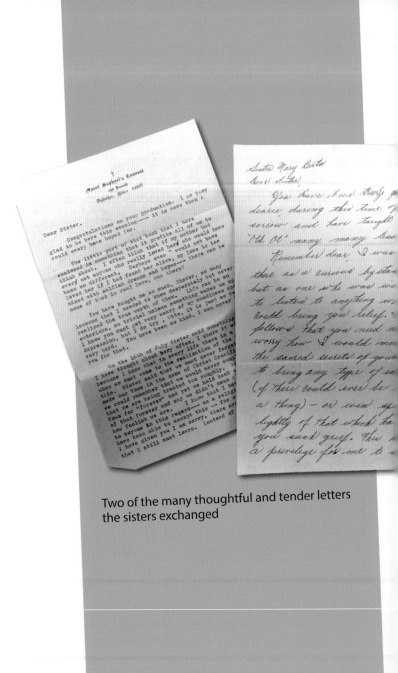

Two of the many thoughtful and tender letters the sisters exchanged

anything between meals and also try with all my power not to give in at all at biting my nails. I have told God I will take any part of this suffering and maybe just the awful lonesomeness being here and trying to put on a good front is a share in your deep lonesomeness, etc.

Berta buddy please do come to Dubuque soon! Every afternoon we could go swimming and maybe this might help to relax you even a tiny bit. You are working probably too hard.

…Please do write again and no pretending. I want to know everything—don't think I worry. No—I just pray harder. Tis true, there is a deep concern which is my privilege to have for you.

Keep trying—you are so good!

Love and prayers,

Sr. Otto, BVM

The sisters were still apart when the mother Sr. Berta had despaired of ever seeing came back to her life—but with a jolt of pain instead of comfort.

LOSING MOTHER, TWICE

In January 1964, Sr. Berta learned that her mother had tried to commit suicide by taking an overdose of sleeping pills. An ambulance brought her to Cook County Hospital, an urban teaching hospital. She survived, but just barely. Cecelia had been living at the Clarendon Hotel at 4520 North Clarendon.

It had been more than two decades since Berta had seen her mother.

The knowledge of her mother's suicide attempt shook Sr. Berta deeply. According to the Catholic teachings, suicide was a gravely wrong, immoral action that violated a love of oneself and one's family and friends and defied the love one owed God.

Sr. Berta was also angry at the pain her mother must have caused her grandmother. The hotel where Cecelia lived was only four miles from her mother's home. Sr. Berta felt caught between her grandmother and her mother.

According to letters between the sisters, it appears Sr. Berta did confide what happened to a select few nuns, including Sr. Otto. She received letters of consolation and support. Sr. Mary Rose Esther told her, "No mother loved a daughter more completely than I love you." A few letters suggest she may have visited her mother and that she and her grandmother may have made some attempt to care for Cecelia.

Perhaps one of her confidantes reminded her that the Catechism allows that:

Grave psychological disturbances, anguish, or grave fear of hardship, suffering, or torture can diminish the responsibility of the one committing suicide" (#2282). This qualification does not make suicide a right action in any circumstance; however, it does make us realize that the person may not be totally culpable for the action because of various circumstances or personal conditions.

Sr. Berta seemed to soften when a friend of her mother's, Al Boldt, sketched the sad details of Cecelia's life. Her mother had gotten involved with a boy from the neighborhood, Tom McBride, around the time of Sr. Berta's birth. She then left home for good in 1944 with Red Arand. His parents were close friends of Sr. Berta's grandmother. In 1957, Cecelia met and married Edward John Dawson. She suffered bleeding ulcers and underwent surgery for them. Then her husband passed away on November 9, 1963, only two months before Cecelia attempted suicide. Sr. Berta wrote a note expressing her gratitude to Al:

Dear Al,

I feel as if I have known you for a very long time after these last weeks.

I am grateful to you for being so good to my mother over all these years. You were certainly there when she needed you the most.

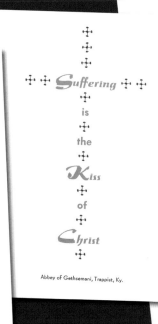

✠
✠
✠
✠ ✠ *Suffering* ✠ ✠
✠
is
✠
the
✠
Kiss
✠
of
✠
Christ
✠

Abbey of Gethsemani, Trappist, Ky.

TO LIVE IS CHRIST TO DIE IS GAIN
ST PAUL

Some of the Mass cards Sr. Berta received after her mother passed away

Thank you too for your kindness to me over these last couple of weeks. It meant so much to me to hear you talk about her. I feel as if I know her a little bit after hearing the things you said about her.

Thank you again for everything, Al.

Gratefully,

Sister Berta, BVM

On May 2, 1964, Cecelia Dawson suffered a heart attack that she did not survive. Weiss Memorial Hospital pronounced her "dead on arrival." She was 52 years old.

Her mother's death now became public. It inspired an outpouring of sympathy from Sr. Berta's fellow nuns, family friends, and parishioners at St. Jerome. The head of the BVM order wrote:

Dear Sister,

As each day passes I hope that you can more easily find your Mother in the loving embrace of Our Lord. It is likely that you still grieve for her and God is permitting that so as to bring both of you closer to Him, you in your earthly abode and her in the heavenly one. Be sure to trust God more and more each day, and prove your love for Him by complete resignation and abandonment. I am enclosing a Mass offering which you may wish to use for your Mother. Affectionately yours, Mother Mary Consolatrice, BVM

A Father Rosemeyer from the Collegio Santa Maria Del Lago in Rome sent a tender letter to Sr. Berta's grandmother dated June 15, 1964, promising to offer Mass for her:

The fact that you have asked me to pray for her is, in a way, a prayer that you yourself are saying for her, so I know that deep down in your own heart you have forgiven her, just as you tell Our Lord that you do every time you say the Our Father.

Nothing would please me more than to have you tell Our Lord the next time that you receive Him that you forgive her and that you want to offer up the sufferings of those twenty years for the good of her soul.

Sr. Berta struggled to forgive her mother. She contributed money toward Mass stipends "for the repose of the soul of Cecelia Sailer Dawson" to Father Joseph Griffin in Ames, Iowa.

The records show that the BVM motherhouse sent Sr. Berta to Saint Raphael's convent in Dubuque for several weeks, perhaps to deal with her grief. Sr. Otto, who was at Clarke College, wrote her encouraging letters, filled with gentle counsel. In one she says:

Dear Sister,

Needless to say, you must know I have been thinking about you frequently these days—especially in the afternoons and late nights. My prayer is the same—not for God to remove the cross, but for His continued grace and strength for you to carry the cross. Are you? Don't underestimate your efforts dear. They too should give you courage.

In another letter, Sr. Otto says:

Dear Sister,

You have been truly great, dearie, during this time of sorrow and have taught "Old Ot" many, many lessons. This has been a privilege for me to be able to be close to a person who has been <u>definitely chosen</u> by God to help carry a <u>hand-picked</u> cross for Him.

…Keep your heart open to Him—accepting all the daily graces and aid which He will never cease offering to you. Only we ourselves can close God off—a frightening thought—but true. Love never forces itself on anyone. Hang on to Him—even though you feel completely abandoned.

You do see the necessity of daily Communion even during <u>our most desperate</u> temptations—humiliating as they might be. Be one of the FIRST to receive Him. God will lead you and help you in <u>some</u> way I know. The only disappointment would be if you should deliberately disappoint Him—and you won't if you but <u>trust.</u> God is too good to be outdone in His love and generosity. Do continue to stay with Him.

God love you.

Lovingly,

Sister Otto

Perhaps "Old Ot" feared her friend was moving away from a God-centered life. Sr. Berta's reply must have comforted her. It arrived soon after on July 30, 1964, the day Sr. Otto graduated with a bachelor of arts degree. The letter included a passage from *That Man Is You*, by Louis Evely:

Behind men's grumpiest poses and most puzzling defense mechanisms—respectability and seriousness, arrogance, silence, or cursing, He could see a child who hadn't been loved enough and who'd stopped developing because someone had ceased believing in him.

Appearances never fooled Him; He knew that people try to look wicked as well as good and that both kinds are equally piteous. We've become so evil because no one has

COLLEGIO S. MARIA DEL LAGO
VIA SARDEGNA, 44
ROMA

June 15, 1964

Dear Bertha,

First of all, I want to tell you how sorry I am about your daughter. I will offer Mass for her, and for you, before the end of the month.

The fact that you have asked me to pray for her is, in a way, a prayer that you yourself are saying for her, so I know that deep down in your own heart you have forgiven her, just as you tell Our Lord that you do every time you say the Our Father.

Nothing would please me more than to have you tell Our Lord the next time that you receive Him that you forgive here and that you want to offer up the sufferings of those twenty years for the good of her soul.

Please give my best regards to Sister Bernadita and the others. I just received word that she has been transferred from St. Jerome's, and I know how very much she will be missed there.

In Christ,

Fr. Rosenmeyer

A condolence letter from Father Rosenmeyer, Sr. Berta's childhood priest *loved us or discovered the real us, because no one has inspired us or wanted us to be better. Inside of every human being God exists and waits to be detected so that He may thrive.*

....Since people don't have the courage to mature unless someone has faith in them, we have to reach those we meet at the level where they stopped developing, where they were given up as hopeless and so withdrew into themselves and began to secrete a protective shell because they thought no one cared. They have to feel they're loved very deeply and very boldly before they dare appear humble and kind, affectionate, sincere, and vulnerable.

So many snarl or stay aloof or try desperately to be repulsive.... How thirsty they must have been to become so hard. How they must have suffered to become so bad. And how we must console them for all those wrongs.

The letter she enclosed reads:

Dear Sister,

...I often think that if my mother had ever met anyone who really loved her she would have been so different. Perhaps even I could not have loved her, my love is too mixed with selfish dreams and hopes—there can be none of that in real love, can there?

...Life can be so trivial unless something wakes us up. I know you must get very weary of my moodiness and depression, but I do try, Otto. It is just so very, very hard.

...We must never forget that we made our Vows in the name of Christ Crucified, if only we could remember that we would never complain or feel that we are being treated too roughly...I know that I have been no example to anyone in this regard—as a religious, I should have been able to accept this—for any bad example I have given you I am sorry.

There are many lessons that I still must learn. Instead of carrying this Cross, I spend every moment trying to put it down or give it to someone else. Please pray Otto that I may be more worthy of the privilege which is mine and stop trying to hide from what is expected of me.

Sr. Corita's sixth-grade class at Our Lady of the Angels

You know, Otto, God has refused many things in my life, but He has been very generous in the wonderful people He has put there. I thank God every day for the opportunity of knowing you and calling you my friend, for you have certainly proved yourself in every regard...

Your loving,

Sr. Berta, BVM

Despite reference to her vows, when Sr. Berta returned to Our Lady of the Angels convent, she began to shift away from thinking about God in capital letters and toward improving the lives of the lowercase humans around her. Saving lives took precedence over saving souls. She got more daring in cooking up fun activities for the children in their free time. Sr. Otto marveled at her determination:

I admired Sr. Berta for her attitude that nothing is too hard that it can't be done. She will tackle anything, and she's willing to stick with it to the bitter end. She will not take no for an answer. You don't say to her, "I'll do it tomorrow." You do it now. Now means NOW. Tomorrow may never come is her attitude.

Sr. Berta appreciated Sr. Otto's calm:

Some people are real, and some are phonies. She was quiet and thoughtful, but we had fun together too. We ate our supper together and laughed about the antics of some of the other sisters. Sister James Aloysius, in particular, kept a bowlful of tennis balls on her desk. She'd fire them at kids who got out of line. She had a fast pitch and great aim. She was a huge lady and was always hiding food. She squirreled it away to her room. We'd say, "There goes Sr. James with a roast to her roost."

COMING OUT OF THE CONVENT

Sr. Berta's turn toward the business of everyday life mirrored a profound transformation under way among women religious and the Catholic Church. Pope John XXIII had opened the Second Vatican Council of the Roman Catholic Church to order on October 11, 1962, for the purpose of promoting spiritual renewal and modernizing the church. What shape this would take was the subject of much debate in convents like Our Lady of the Angels. While many older nuns feared change, Srs. Berta and Otto both welcomed it.

Nuns around the country came out of their habits, their convents, and the cloisters into the community. Liberation from total dependence on a mother superior to prescribe their every action was in the air. Sr. Otto says:

Nuns were just starting to go out at night, mingling with people in the evening. The role of nuns and what they could do was changing. It was the dawn of nuns as activists. We are here to go out and help people. Many people thought nuns should just stay in convents and pray, but we wanted to do. Everything you do can be a prayer.

"We are here for the people," Sr. Otto said one night at dinner. "If we aren't helping people, why are we here?" The two sisters thought reaching out to the children would be a good way to aid in the salvation of some of the teens in the neighborhood. Both had become fiercely protective of the kids and determined that they should have opportunities to enjoy themselves. It seemed a natural next step to Srs. Berta and Otto to resurrect the teen club.

They requested a meeting with the OLA administrator, Monsignor Joseph Cussen.

"These children have nowhere to go," Sr. Berta said. "If they had a safe place to hang out, they wouldn't cause so much trouble."

Monsignor Cussen agreed to let the two sisters reopen The Hall for a teen club.

"They are the best kids," said Sr. Otto with a beatific smile of absolute certainty. "They wouldn't think of hurting us."

Those nuns did everything for us. How they took all we dished out is beyond me. They were all saints.

—Bob Johncola, former OLA student

The sisters soon showed themselves capable of mischief, despite assertions of goodness, when they ventured out with the teens Sr. Berta says:

The convent had one old station wagon that we could reserve for things like going to the doctor. Only about six of the three dozen nuns could drive. So, the car was often available. We'd get the key to the garage where the car was kept and drive to Hardee's to get a hamburger. Then we started taking kids to the Art Institute of Chicago, to ball games at Wrigley Field, and to the Shedd Aquarium.

One day, we were driving down the Dan Ryan Expressway with 12 teenagers crammed in the back. Sr. Otto was driving, and I was in the front seat. A kid named Victor crawled out the back window of the wagon to the roof. He managed to scoot himself to the front and hang over the windshield. He scared us to death.

Occasionally, we let a teenager stay in the basement of the convent, and we didn't tell if these kids didn't have a place to go. Are you going to put out a No Vacancy sign for a kid?

While most of the other nuns turned in by 8:00 p.m., Srs. Berta and Otto took some of the neighborhood kids to cultural events. The nuns in the convent frowned on their nocturnal activities, but the two paid little attention to the approbation. Running the teen center would keep them out even later, but it would extend their outreach as well.

CLUB RULES

Their first order of business was to expand the hours. The center used to close at 6:00 p.m. The sisters kept it open until midnight. They encouraged the kids who hung out there to bring their friends. They had no trouble keeping order. Sr. Otto says:

Most of the kids who hung out here were boys. We never had any fear. It was a pretty rowdy club, but we never had a problem. We told them, "We are here for you to have a good time. We want you to have fun, not be disruptive. The rules are "No drinking. No cursing."

We'd hear, "Shhh, the nuns are around," whenever we walked into the room. We knew trouble was brewing.

The kids would get an adult to buy liquor for them on Chicago Avenue, and they tried to sneak bottles into the hall, so we took the bottles away from them. We hid them in the water tank of the toilet in a bathroom that we kept locked. We took a little home with us.

The Hall, home of the West Side Jokers

The Spanish Club started by the sisters at Our Lady of the Angels

The boys talked about planning fights with other gangs, and we paid close attention. When we heard them mention dates and times, we called the police. The kids never figured out how the police always knew about their fights. "Dang," they'd say. "The police were there, again." The kids had gloves with nails, brass knuckles, and clubs. They fought with those. Even the girls put tacks in their gloves and got into fights, but no one had guns.

John Pellettiere was a Teen Club member. He lived right across the street from Our Lady of the Angels. His parents were active in the congregation. He says:

The neighbors didn't like the kids who congregated in front of The Hall. We smoked, took furtive sips from flasks that we hid in our back pockets, and listened to rock and roll music. I ran around with the West Side Jokers. We all got picked up by the local police. We were juvenile delinquents.

Sr. Berta took some flak from the neighbors because we congregated outside. She provided a place for us to go. She was a wonderful lady, very friendly, warm, and welcoming, but when we got rowdy and crazy, she put us in our place.

Puddles protected the sisters from harm. Sr. Berta had adopted a German shepherd mix and trained him to relieve himself on a piece of carpet outside the front door of the convent, so she wouldn't have to walk him long distances through the rough neighborhood at night. He accompanied her everywhere and was fiercely protective. The kids at The Hall were wary of him, which helped keep order. Keeping the kids busy worked too. The sisters ramped up activities for the members. Sr. Berta says:

The Hall was a place for us to go. If it wasn't there, God knows what would have happened to us.

—John Pellettiere, former OLA student and retired CFO of Sunrise Medical

John Pellettiere on his high school graduation day in 1964

When we took over the club, there were only a few decks of cards and a television set. We talked people into donating stuff. Soon we had a jukebox and a speed-punching bag. I kept saying I wished we had a pool table. One day, a person with a heavy Italian accent called the club and said, "Sister, one day a pool table will come in an unmarked truck. You are not to ask any questions. You are not to even talk to the guys who set it up." The secret caller was right. One day, we got an absolutely gorgeous pool table with a slate top. The deliverymen put it together. We told the boys not to say anything to them. I never found out who gave it to us.

A YMCA camp in Michigan offered to let the sisters bring several kids from The Hall—in the middle of winter. John Pellettiere was one of the campers:

We went out at night and started a bonfire that got out of control. We ended up burning down quite a few pine trees. If snow hadn't been on the ground, we would have burned the place down. The local fire department had to come to put out the fire. We were wild and crazy.

While one group was setting fires outside, another was doing the same inside, desperately trying to stay warm and well. Sr. Berta says:

We had four cabins with no heat. Temperatures went down to zero. The kids got some wood and started a fire in the fireplace. They ran out of wood and burned some furniture to keep us warm. The second night, Victor was running a high fever. We took him to the hospital, and a doctor said he had a bad case of strep throat. He told us we had to make all the kids go out in the cold while we aired out the cabins. He taught me how to give Victor penicillin shots. When we got back to Chicago, I went to his house and gave him a shot every day. The kids had a good time.

Sr. Berta became known as a loose cannon around the parish. Even she seemed to recognize her own rambunctiousness. In an undated note to herself in Chicago, she typed:

SLOW ME DOWN, LORD!
EASE THE POUNDING OF MY HEART
BY THE QUIETING OF MY MIND!

Back in Chicago, she scouted for new ways to entertain the kids. She took a group of them to rent motorcycles—something the parents weren't too happy about when they found out.

Around 1966, Sr. Berta approached Father Patrick F. Kelly, the administrator of Our Lady of the Angels, to sponsor a softball team with

OUR LADY OF THE ANGELS SCHOOL
3814 WEST IOWA STREET
CHICAGO 51, ILLINOIS

SLOW ME DOWN, LORD!
EASE THE POUNDING OF MY HEART
BY THE QUIETING OF MY MIND!

One of Sr. Berta's notes to self

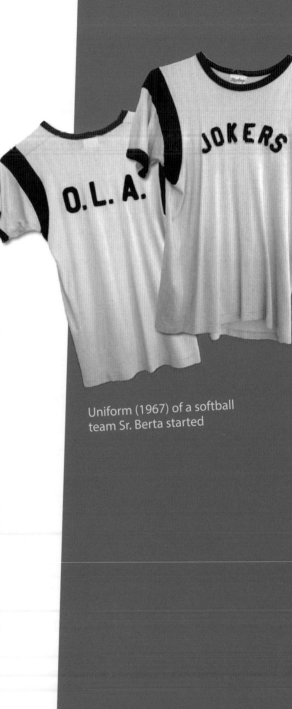

Uniform (1967) of a softball team Sr. Berta started

members from The Hall. There was a softball league at LaFollette Park, about three miles from Our Lady of the Angels.

Father Kelly replaced Monsignor Cussen, who had suffered a stroke the previous year. A former Navy chaplain, Father Kelly wasn't as soft a touch as his predecessor, but Sr. Berta prevailed. She also convinced him to pay for the team's uniforms. It would be one of his last acts of generosity toward the Teen Club. The team called itself The Jokers.

Sr. Berta drove the boys, clad in their bright-yellow shirts, to the park for games, and she cheered from the sidelines. On the way home, she took the rowdy bunch for hamburgers.

Sr. Berta soon got into trouble for providing this shuttle service. She says:

When the mother superior found out what we were doing, she changed the lock on the garage. So I called someone at a nearby brewery, and they donated an old station wagon to The Hall, so we had our own car. We could go anywhere we wanted, and we didn't let the convent use it. That didn't make the new mother superior happy either.

Sr. Berta was always ready to push the boundaries. The principal of the school, Sr. Mary Rose Esther, BVM, had passed away on November 21, 1966. She had been a source of great encouragement to Sr. Berta and especially to Sister Otto, who often despaired when she had to teach subjects, like math, that made her uncomfortable. The new principal was made of sterner stuff and was less tolerant of the younger nuns.

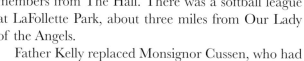

I've always had a hard time with crazy rules.

—Sr. Berta

West Side Jokers team circa 1968
(Photo courtesy of Gary Rushton)

The once tranquil Humboldt Park neighborhood of the 1890s had become known for crime and gang violence by the 1960s (Photo courtesy of Chicago Transit Authority)

LET IT ALL HANG OUT

Most of the families in the neighborhood didn't have television sets. Since there was one at The Hall, the place was packed with people to watch the first contest between the champions of the National Football League and the new American Football League on January 15, 1967. (This contest would become known as Super Bowl I.) The NFL's Green Bay Packers faced the AFL's Kansas City Chiefs at the Los Angeles Memorial Coliseum in California. The temperature was a sunny 72 degrees at the stadium. In Chicago, it was a gray, chilly day, just over 10 degrees.

Inside, the kids buzzed with talk about their favorite players and debated whether the Packers' Bart Starr was a better quarterback than the Chiefs' Len Dawson. They made bets on the outcome. Just minutes before kickoff, Srs. Berta and Otto showed up at The Hall and took off their coats.

They were wearing something no one had ever seen them wear before—street clothes. The appearance of two nuns in black jackets and skirts that revealed their ankles stunned the jabbering boys into silence.

The BVM order had been debating whether to make the scratchy, floor-length, wool habits optional. Habits were not part of the founders' original vision. Along the way, to oblige church hierarchy, the order had adopted a habit code. In 1967, the order decided to return to the original spirit, which allowed members to dress in contemporary style. Therefore, the sisters decided to see what it felt like.

The crowd at The Hall couldn't have been more shocked had they seen the two sisters run out onto the Memorial Coliseum field in football uniforms.

"Holy shit!" said one.

"Shhh," said another. "You know we don't cuss in front of da nuns."

For the first time, the boys realized the sisters were *women*—like their mothers, sisters, and, even worse, girlfriends.

"We freaked out," John Pellettiere said. "All of a sudden, it was like, who are these people? They looked like ladies. No one wanted to look at them."

Their habit-less attire also shocked the other nuns and some of the priests at Our Lady of the Angels. One more example of their daring went on the negative side of their ledger with the church leadership—along with regular complaints from neighbors about the rowdy Teen Club.

Peeved at the free-spirited nuns, Father Kelly must have seen his opportunity when he began a review of the church's finances to look for ways to lower expenses. His review included his intentions to shutter some of the church properties on Hamlin Avenue.

The first one he ordered closed was The Hall. The sisters were deeply disappointed and suspected that their days at Our Lady of the Angels were numbered. They wondered what June 1967 would bring, when the BVM motherhouse would notify members of their assignments for the coming year.

Not long after closing The Hall, Father Kelly announced plans to build a new teen center. According to an article in the July 20, 1967, edition of the *Chicago Tribune*, the parish had recently purchased two properties for this purpose on Hamlin Avenue—across the street from the shuttered teen club. A resident in the area called the idea "a dream come true," claiming, "It has been a 24-hour job keeping my children from going into gangs because there was no place they were allowed to congregate."

The new center would be called Kelly Hall.

Official BVM order that sent
Sr. Corita to Kansas City

KANSAS CITY BOUND

Sr. Otto had been teaching at Our Lady of the Angels for more than nine years when the BVM motherhouse sent her walking papers. A letter dated June 1, 1967, read:

My dear Sister,

You have been elected Local Superior of St. Vincent Convent, Kansas City, Missouri. You know that this is an important and challenging work for the Community during this period of growth and development within the Church. I am confident that, with God's help, you will fulfill your duties with an awareness that the superior's assignment is one of loving service to others and that a humble spirit finds the key to the confidence and joy which mark a religious house.

Please write to me at once, dear Sister, indicating your acceptance of this assignment…

May God bless you, my dear Sister.
Your devoted,
Mother Mary Consolatrice, BVM

The assignment was a promotion. As local superior, Sr. Otto would be the principal of the school at St. Vincent de Paul, a struggling inner-city parish run by Vincentian fathers that the diocese hoped to close. She would be replacing Sister Frances Irene, who had only served two years in the position. That might make the transition easier.

Sr. Otto had a sister in Kansas City, and she felt lucky. Another letter from the BVM motherhouse ordered one of the other OLA nuns to report to Bogotá, Colombia.

This year's assignment was different from all the others. It gave Sr. Otto the option of refusing. It was also the first time her birth name, Corita, appeared in BVM correspondence. She would leave behind both her identity as Otto and her dear friend.

Sr. Corita arrived in Kansas City in August 1967. The United States sent 45,000 troops to Vietnam that month. The Beatles song "All You Need Is Love" topped the charts, and U.S. Congress was considering whether to confirm Thurgood Marshall as the first African-American U.S. Supreme Court Justice.

The "summer of love" that birthed flower children, the hippie revolution, and a burst of rebellious creativity was still blazing when Sr. Corita stood in front of the august, Georgian-style school building at 3104 Flora. Made of Carthage limestone, the building appeared to be in fine shape. The diocese had built it in 1906 as a charter school, one of the first fireproof Catholic schools in the country, according to Louis Tofari, historian for St. Vincent de Paul and communicator for the Society for Saint Pius X (SSPX).

Sr. Corita climbed the nine front steps and looked down a long, dark hallway with classrooms on either side. She was about to become part of a movement that would affect society, the Catholic Church, and, more immediately, the neighborhood around her new parish.

She thought of how she would describe the place in a letter to Sr. Berta back at Our Lady of the Angels in Chicago, more than 500 miles away.

St. Vincent's Academy in Kansas City

CHAPTER 4
A SNAKE IN THE CLASS

At first, 13-year-old Kim Randolph thought gremlins had staged a pillow fight when she gazed down the long central hallway. A carpet of feathers covered the floor, and thousands still wafted in the air.

Chickens for the science class sometimes escaped from their roosts in the gymnasium and roamed around the school. Their clucking was usually the first greeting Kim got when she arrived before school to feed the menagerie of animals at St. Vincent de Paul Academy in Kansas City. She didn't hear a peep on this day in 1971.

The creatures in residence today included a pair of alligators called Bonnie and Clyde, a few rabbits, a bathtub full of frogs, a dozen or so chickens, and an eight-foot-long boa constrictor, aptly named Boa.

Kim was delighted to hang out at St. Vincent's, where she'd been a student since 1968. She went to confession and to Mass, where she took communion, even though her family was Methodist.

Kim Randolph felt more comfortable at St. Vincent's than she did in her own home. Her father was stationed overseas in the U.S. Air Force. Her mother worked two jobs, so she dropped Kim off at 6:00 a.m. each morning, two hours before the school day started. Kim hung out at the convent nearby and helped the sisters. Feeding the animals was one of her favorite tasks.

A tennis-ball-size knot formed in her throat as she crept slowly down the hall. Near the end of the hallways where the animal cages sat, she saw Boa curled up *outside* his cage.

She saw the bulge in the snake's ordinarily forearm-wide girth and screamed, "Sr. Berta, Sr. Berta, I think Boa ate a chicken!"

Children at the recently revamped school didn't need textbooks anymore to learn about the cycle of life.

Kim Randolph

SOMETHING'S HAPPENING HERE

Math class

The parochial school for children in first through eighth grades was once a staid bastion of Catholic education. Sisters in starched habits rapped knuckles and swatted behinds to ensure orderly classrooms. Children sat in neat grids with their hands clasped and hearts pounding, for fear of incurring the wrath of their teachers, whose hooded habits made them resemble raptors. Many of the nuns were as skillful as hawks at swooping down on their students.

Sister Peggy's math tutelage still inspired terror among the hearts of addled adders. Sum up two plus two as five, and the penalty would be reciting a few Hail Marys for the mistake. This old-school nun, though, was fast becoming the exception at this inner-city school southeast of downtown Kansas City.

In the four years since the BVM order had sent Sr. Corita to St. Vincent's, she had turned the school upside down and done exactly what she was not supposed to do.

In 1967, the Diocese of Kansas City-St. Joseph had asked the BVM motherhouse in Dubuque, Iowa, for a candidate to run the St. Vincent de Paul Academy, *temporarily.*

Enrollment, once more than 200 students, had dropped to 95. Only four out of more than a dozen classrooms were in use. The Vincentian priests running the parish had been borrowing from the diocese to keep the church itself open and owed the diocese about $50,000 according to *This Far By Faith*, a history of parishes in the Kansas City area, by Charles M. Coleman.

The diocese hoped to consolidate under-performing parish schools like St. Vincent's. The leadership of the diocese hoped the new principal would smooth the path to shut down the school.

The neighborhood around St. Vincent's was in transition. It had been largely comprised of working-class Catholic families of European descent. There were Germans, Irish, and Italians who worked as mechanics and

When we first came to Kansas City, there were no food pantries. There were no shelters. Our families were poor, but they had the basics—unlike now.

—Sr. Berta

shopkeepers. Up until the 1960s, most of the kids lived in two-parent families. Sr. Corita estimated that only 10 percent of the children lived in single-parent households when she arrived. However, the neighborhood's original population had aged, and newcomers were increasingly black.

The race riots that occurred in the wake of Martin Luther King's assassination in Memphis on April 4, 1968, shook Kansas City. School districts all over the country called off classes in honor of King's funeral, set for April 9. The Kansas City School District was one of the few that did not. A large group of teenagers protested at City Hall, and a local disc jockey invited them to a dance at a nearby church, Holy Name. The police, unaware of the dance and fearing a riot, responded to a call about a disturbance there. Some of the teenagers threw stones at the police, who responded with tear gas. When the young people ran inside, police fired six canisters of tear gas into the church basement, affecting about 400 teenagers and their chaperones.

Intermittent skirmishes broke out for months afterward. Father James Lawbaugh, an associate pastor at St. Vincent's who was white, was crossing Linwood Boulevard to visit one of the parish families when a carful of black teenagers threw a Molotov cocktail at him and screamed, "You honky priest, if you don't get your ass out of here, you'll be next!"

Father Lawbaugh had been at a priest conference in Perryville, Missouri, with the head pastor, Father McKinley, when he learned of King's assassination. St. Vincent's was his first assignment after his ordination in 1966. In just two years, he had grown attached to the hard-working families in the neighborhood. He left the conference immediately to drive back to Kansas City. Dozens of fires, visible for miles outside the city, made him feel like he was entering a war zone. Father McKinley never came back. Father James P. Cashman

Father James Lawbaugh

replaced him as pastor, but he didn't last long.

Priests started leaving the parish, just like parishioners. When Sr. Corita arrived, there were five priests serving the congregation. Fewer than two years later, there were two: Reverend John O'Malley Sharpe and Father Lawbaugh.

Sr. Corita quickly realized that the school curriculum developed for the

Mixed-age St. Vincent's classroom

Irish and Italian Catholic parish didn't resonate with the black children, who were mostly from Baptist homes. The newcomers were poorer, more likely to live in single-parent households, and in need of more services. When she arrived in 1967, the congregation was more than 60 percent white, as was the school. By 1969, the school was about 85 percent black.

A natural fixer, Sr. Corita wanted the school to be more responsive to students and to put more of the three-story building to use, beyond just four classrooms. During her first year as principal, she tried having teachers change classrooms instead of the students. The nuns made an effort, but they were older and set in their ways.

For the 1968-69 academic year, Sr. Corita wanted to reorganize the school. She had an idea to group students by their abilities instead of their ages, but she would need teachers who were more pliable and willing to try new teaching techniques.

WITHER THOU GOEST

In the wake of the Second Vatican Council, nuns were gaining more control over their destinies. In 1968, the Catholic Church allowed women religious to choose where they wanted to go. Sr. Corita thought of Sr. Berta. She had heard that her friend was in trouble and increasingly isolated in Chicago, so she called her at the Our Lady of the Angels convent.

"You have to come help me," Sr. Corita said. "I need you. Would you be willing to teach the seventh- and eighth-grade classes in Kansas City?"

Sr. Berta says:

Kansas City wasn't that far from my grandma in Chicago. Our Lady of the Angels was a big place. With 35 nuns, some are going to be sane, and some aren't. The OLA convent was very conservative. When I came out of the habit there, that made the conservative ones angry. Some of the priests there were against the changes. It was appealing to go to a smaller place and try something new.

Sr. Corita described the families in the neighborhood and all the church was doing for them. She talked about one of the priests, Father James Lawbaugh, and his outreach efforts in the neighborhood. He had been holding ice cream socials.

Sr. Mary Rose Esther, who had been so supportive of Sr. Berta, had passed away, and the new priest at Our Lady of the Angels had closed the Teen Club. Sr. Berta was facing more criticism of her relaxed teaching style too. The thought of reuniting with her friend made the offer even more appealing.

"It sounds good," Sr. Berta said. "Besides, I've never been to Kansas City before."

Sr. Berta arrived in June 1968 with her dog, Puddles, and all of her worldly goods in a black-leather steamer trunk that weighed 58 pounds. Protests and demonstrations related to the assassination of Martin Luther King, Jr. were still erupting around the area. Civil rights activists were mobilizing. Bernard Powell and others formed the Social Action Committee of 20 (SAC-20) to teach leadership skills to young blacks.

Sr. Berta, who had been used to the Irish and Italian families in Chicago, had trouble understanding black dialect. After two weeks in Kansas City, she told Sr. Corita, "I can't stay here anymore. I can't understand what anyone is saying."

"Be patient," Corita counseled. "You'll get it."

Sr. Berta soon won over the students and their parents with her exuberance, imagination, and sense of humor. She was meeting with a group of prospective volunteers at the school when one asked her if she had trouble with any of the Catholic Church's doctrines.

"I have trouble with all the doctrines," she replied.

She and Father Lawbaugh were soon planning block parties and carnivals for the neighborhood. Sr. Berta arranged pony rides for 15 cents. She got an extra-long extension cord and brought the record player out to the street. Songs like "Spinning Wheel," "Sugar, Sugar," "Aquarius," "Honky Tonk Women," and "I Can't Get Next to You" blared on Flora, while the kids danced and enjoyed the fare, usually Kool-Aid, Jell-O, and cookies. At one such event, Sr. Berta baked a red cake in the shape of an aardvark.

Word of the high spirits spread.

UN-NUNS IN THE CONVENT

Nineteen-year-old Claudia York had the complexion of an English tea rose and the determination of Torquemada to make the world a better place. She ran away from her home in Kentucky when her old-fashioned father didn't want her to go to college. She arrived in Kansas City in February 1969 and needed a job and a place to live. Someone who volunteered at St. Vincent's told her about the sisters.

The sisters were impressed with her determined stance, fine mind, and musical abilities. So, they offered her a job for $50 a month, plus room and board.

Claudia coached the basketball team, ran for supplies, played guitar for Mass, and was always ready to do the sisters' bidding. She helped Father Lawbaugh with recreational programs.

She worked with Father Lawbaugh to get a grant for a pool table from the Office of Economic Opportunities. When Vernon Thompson from OEO came to check on the pool table, the cheeky Claudia asked him for money to run a summer program.

She wrote a grant and got $2,900. It paid for St. Vincent's teachers to oversee playground games, picnics, swimming excursions, and field trips to Fairyland Park and the Kansas City Zoo.

Claudia was the first layperson to move into the convent with the sisters, but she wouldn't be the last. The squat, two-story building had plenty of room.

Claudia York

FROM THE COURT TO THE CLASSROOM

Rich Koch had just graduated from Siena College, then an all-male school in Loudonville, New York, with an economics degree when the United States Army ordered him to report for a physical. He applied for status as a selective conscientious objector (CO) to the Vietnam War. When the local draft board turned down his request, his father hired a lawyer from the firm of William Kunstler. While the case moved through the legal system, he started looking for service jobs to fulfill the CO requirement.

Some of his friends were heading to Nevada, Missouri, on a mission for The Society of Our Lady of the Most Holy Trinity (SOLT), which sent young adults on missions at various locations across the United States and abroad. There were 110 volunteers, and only five of them were men. The odds sounded good to Rich. He loaded up his 10-year-old Volkswagen Beetle and headed to his first posting at Amarillo, Texas. Air conditioning was a hole in the floor; cruise control was a brick on the pedal.

When the Amarillo assignment ended, Rich drove to Kansas City in December 1969 to pick up three more volunteers. To make room in his Beetle, he left his possessions at the SOLT house at 31st and Flora. It happened to be next to the St. Vincent's playground. After a car accident back east totaled his car, he took a bus back to Kansas City in January 1970, to pick up his possessions, and decided to stay. He started practicing his moves on the playground's basketball court.

Sr. Corita sized up the wiry young man with a mop of dark hair darting around the basketball court and wondered if he might be useful in her great experiment in education.

When he asked her why he never saw the kids playing basketball, she said the school didn't have anyone to teach them.

"Would you like to be a basketball coach and teacher at our school?" she said. "You could live in the rectory."

He told her he lacked the certification to be a teacher.

"When you hear what we can pay you, it won't matter."

Twenty young faces ranging in age from six to 12 looked up at Rich as he began his first day as a math teacher at St. Vincent's. Some looked wary and cautious, but most bubbled with mirth.

He introduced himself and told them to call him Mister Rich. He preferred his first name, but Sr. Corita told him he would need to command their respect.

He began with roll call. They dutifully called out their names for him: "Mark Young," "Andrea Young," "Barry Toms," "Winona Jennings," "Kevin Rollins," "Ivory Snow."

Later that day, Sr. Corita pulled him aside discreetly and told him, "I saw your attendance roster. Ivory Snow is laundry detergent. That student's name is Dwayne Ivory Bradford. Don't let them snow you."

Dwayne, who came to St. Vincent's as a third grader in 1967, was an altar boy, but he had a rambunctious side.

"I was pretty naïve," Rich admits. Still, he connected with the kids and soon added a science class to his duties. He continues:

My science classroom was a little wild. We did lots of experiments. One of my favorites was dropping soft-boiled eggs out the window. We took bets on whether they would break. We'd blow things up and heat up cans until they exploded. The students loved it.

Dwayne Ivory Bradford, Roxy Smalls, and Bridgett Wreathers

> *St. Vincent's was a protected place, an oasis from American racism. I did not know about discrimination and racism until after I left.*
>
> **—Barry Kountz, alumnus**

> *You would walk in that building, and you could hear a pin drop. The kids were so engaged in what they were doing.*
>
> **—Sr. Corita**

Rich would prove to be radical in his coaching as well, when he took charge of the boys' basketball, girls' volleyball, and co-ed track teams. He would do more for the sports program at St. Vincent's than Vince Lombardi did for the Green Bay Packers.

Everyone at St. Vincent's took on extra tasks in the same way magnets collect iron filings—and they often discovered talents they never would have discovered otherwise. They were all swept away by the energy two sisters brought to the school.

NO SQUARE INCH LEFT BEHIND

In a traditional school, age determines grade, and this process works as long as the students function at similar levels. At St. Vincent's, however, Sr. Corita noticed soon after arriving that there were wide variations among the students' abilities. She wanted more flexibility in the curriculum.

Sr. Corita opened a small learning center and library for students on the second floor. She put educational games and audiotapes in the hall and let children use them without direct teacher supervision.

She was attracted to a progressive movement in elementary education that had begun years before in England. It favored spirited, child-centered classrooms. According to the Education Encyclopedia (*StateUniversity.com*), about 20 percent of British schools had adopted it by the early 1970s. Only half as many United States schools were brave enough to try it.

But St. Vincent's was among them. Within a few years, the two sisters had redefined everything from the curriculum to the classrooms. According to a report likely authored by Sr. Corita, "Exploring Alternatives: A Summer Workshop for Learners:"

In 1970-71, we broke through to the beginning stages of open education. The primary grades (1-3) were separate from the older children because we discovered they were not prepared

Rich Koch

English teacher Mary Bradley

to formulate their own schedules. We added two more classes—sewing and creative writing, which included spelling, writing, and fundamentals of grammar. At this stage, the older students (grades 4-8) began making their own schedules.

The younger students started in a primary room the sisters opened in the basement. They stayed there until they exhibited a basic readiness to learn.

In 1973, third graders joined the older students in choosing their own schedules. The only requirement was that students had to spend 45 minutes each in math and English every day. Then they were free to choose from the other classes in science, reading, writing, art, and sewing. Each student signed a contract to learn specific things.

Students also had access to the learning center and library to pursue other subjects of their own choosing. Like the chickens, they had the freedom to wander around the building. Students often carried hens into class and kept them on their shoulders or laps.

Music often blared from classrooms. The students' favorites were The Stylistics, Jackson 5, The Temptations, The Spinners, Kool and the Gang, Marvin Gaye, and Smokey Robinson.

The teachers worked with students individually, more like mentors and coaches. Students didn't suffer as much from comparison to their classmates as they would have in a traditional environment. For example, the other students wouldn't know that an eighth grader was reading on a second-grade level. Only the teacher knew. Rich says:

Most schools work by putting children of the same age in a classroom. The problem with inner-city schools was there were wide discrepancies in learning. How can you teach children at the same level when some can read and others can't?

Kids who had done poorly at other schools started to learn at St. Vincent's. They loved having control of their destinies and learning the basics through the lens

If you can find something that interests children, you can tap into their potential. Kids don't want to be in trouble. They won't be if you let them lead you to where they want to go.

—Sr. Corita

Farm animals helped children learn to care for others.

of their own interests. Where possible, lessons were experiences. For math, kids measured the playground or played dominoes and Tri-ominos. They learned fractions from cake recipes.

Stephanie Palmer started as a seventh grader at St. Vincent. She looked forward to school every day, even though she had to wear "some of the *ugliest* uniforms ever to be seen on the earth." Her science class incubated eggs laid by chickens at the school. Stephanie thrived by being able to structure her own day.

According to Kim Randolph:

The teachers used a hands-on approach. We learned about nature and reproduction from a rat, fish, turtles, chickens, a goat, a snake, a gerbil, guinea pigs, hamsters, and rabbits. Every class had a component of the basics. We had to learn how to spell and how to measure in science class. In home education, we learned cooking and sewing, which both involved math. Then we'd have a cook-off or a fashion show. Upstairs on the second level there was a gymnasium with a stage. We built a catwalk and sets for plays.

FRUIT FLIES

Kim wanted to wow her classmates with her eighth-grade science fair project. Sr. Berta had suggested experimenting with something related to breeding. Kim says:

I decided to try to breed fruit flies for a science class. To attract them, all I needed was a jar, chopped-up bananas, and cheesecloth. I needed to look at them under the microscope, though, to determine the males from the females. I couldn't get them under a microscope without sedating them. Sr. Berta called Saint Joseph Hospital on Linwood and asked for help putting fruit flies to sleep. She drove me to the hospital.

Student science project

Science fairs, a regular occurrence

I walked into the emergency department, and a nurse pointed me to the operating room. There, a doctor gave me a spray can of ether. It was about five inches tall with a metal screw cap. It had at least two inches of ether in the can.

All of the class gathered around the table. I dunked cotton balls in the can and tried to hold them over the jars of fruit flies. I started to get very woozy. So did the kids around me.

Sr. Corita's office was near the science room. She smelled the ether and came to investigate.

"What…is…going…on…here?" Sr. Corita said with quiet, scary deliberation. She had a look that put the fear of God into us. She shooed us into the hallway for some fresh air. We heard her say, "Berta, what were you thinking? If you can't follow the rules, you can't teach here."

Sr. Corita could intimidate the students but not Sr. Berta.

"You show me where the rule is about ether," she replied.

An upcoming science fair prompted other students to embark on their own projects. Dwayne Bradford raised two alligators, Bonnie and Clyde, from eggs.

Two other students, Kenny Collins and Kevin Boggess, built a chicken coop and incubator to hatch eggs.

"We were in competition with the chicken raisers," Bradford said. "It was a race to see who could learn the most in the least amount of time."

I never did yell, rant, or rage. That took too much energy. Besides, kids will just laugh. If you talk softly, they don't know what you are thinking, and that makes them nervous.

—Sr. Corita

Sr. Berta and Corita are like Abbott and Costello. They are each other's yin and yang. Sr. Berta steps out of the box, and Sr. Corita tries to put her back into one.

—Kim Randolph

> *The sisters could relate to urban kids. They taught me a lot. I am proud to have come from that school.*
>
> —**Dwayne Bradford, school alumnus**

> *The sisters were more than teachers. They were like mothers, aunts, and big sisters. We developed character because of them.*
>
> —**Kim Randolph, school alumna**

CRIME AND CREATIVE PUNISHMENT

Punishments were as creative as the curriculum. Dwayne Bradford was a habitual spit-wad shooter, until Sr. Berta caught him in the act. She threw 100 beans down a flight of stairs and told him he couldn't go home until he found all of them. It took him a couple of hours.

Sabrina Mitchell said her teacher would turn on a tape recorder if she had to leave the room. "Woe to the person whose voice turned up on tape and got sent to Sr. Corita's office." However, when she wanted to join the football team, Sr. Corita let her play.

Discipline problems vanished. Attendance increased. Mothers reported that their kids came home chattering about what they learned each day. Even the kids from juvenile court fared well under this open-education system.

Word spread through the neighborhood about a school where students didn't want to skip class. Parents began to regard St. Vincent's school as a community center, where children could drop by before and after school to participate in such activities as intramural sports. Many parents who weren't Catholic brought their children and even attended services at the church.

The only folks at St. Vincent's who weren't happy were some of the other nuns who were more accustomed to teaching with rulers and paddles. They didn't favor negotiating contracts with 10-year-olds or having to step over chicken droppings on their way to class.

St. Vincent's students worked
at their own pace

CHAPTER 5
DAYCARE EXECS IN PAJAMAS

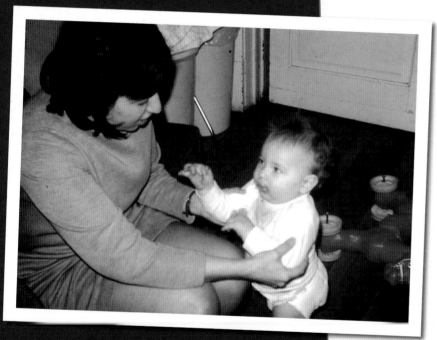

Loving children was at the heart of everything the sisters did

Nuns were disappearing from St. Vincent's. The two-story, brick convent where Berta and Corita lived, at 3121 Paseo, once housed more than 20 sisters. By 1969, only two other nuns lived there.

The Vatican II Council had given nuns the freedom to chart their own courses. As a result, thousands of nuns across the country began to question their calling, and many left the sisterhood altogether. More than 4,300 nuns would leave their orders in the coming year, according to *Double Crossed*, by Kenneth Briggs.

The seminal summer of 1969 tilted the world. President Nixon announced the withdrawal of 25,000 U.S. troops from Vietnam. The Stonewall riots between police and gay bar patrons in New York City ushered in the gay rights movement. Apollo 11 landed on the moon. The British sent troops into Northern Ireland. Charles Manson killed actress Sharon Tate and seven others.

And as the sun set on this seminal summer, the Woodstock music festival brought 400,000 people to a farm in Bethel, New York, on August 15.

The swirling of ideas affected St. Vincent's as well. The new curriculum, wild critters in the classrooms, and more unruly student body started to take their toll on the resident nuns who were used to a more sedate, contemplative life. Two sisters left their order to marry former priests. Other nuns, who could now choose where they wanted to live, decided it wasn't with Puddles.

Puddles, remembering his early training, did not distinguish between indoor and outdoor carpeting. In St. Vincent's convent, the only carpeting was in the chapel, where he peed frequently. Puddles had other annoying traits. He was so possessive over his toys that he bit a few people who tried to pet him as he played with them.

As the nuns departed, they left open positions in the school and empty space in the convent. This fanned Berta's imagination, and she started musing about how to fill the empty places.

One Friday, a mother said to her, "I wish you had a place for the younger kids here, so I could work."

"We have this big house, and it's empty," Sr. Berta told Corita that evening. "Let's turn the convent into a childcare center. We could open on Monday."

"That's impossible," Sr. Corita said.

"No, it isn't."

That was pretty much the extent of the planning. Sr. Berta's good intentions often had to stand in place of planning. Sr. Corita knew it would be pointless to disagree. They both figured they would work things out on the fly.

GARAGE SALE-ING LESSONS

Their first hurdle was a lack of toys and equipment for babies and toddlers. Sr. Berta says:

Over the weekend, Anna Jennings, a parishioner, introduced us to garage sales. She taught us that the farther south we went the better we'd do. When people in the inner city sell clothes, they want to make money, but those in more affluent areas out south just want to get rid of stuff. Mrs. Jennings was a large, formidable woman. She probably weighed 300 pounds and was very dark-skinned.

As they stood in front of their first house on September 6, 1969, Anna Jennings whispered, "They're going to be glad that all I came for was to buy stuff and not to live next door to them. They'll sell cheap." She was right. The two spent the weekend going from sale to sale and came back with cribs, high chairs, and potty chairs. They got baskets full of hot new toys like Upsy Downsy Babies, Zeroids, and Wizzers, along with stuffed bunnies, lions, and lambs—most of which still had two eyes.

Daycare began on a whim with toys from garage sales

When Berta gets an idea, we do it. Thinking comes afterward.

–Sr. Corita

Hubert Rice, the daycare's first customer

When the two told the homeowners they were trying to start a childcare center for the poor, they got some of the stock for free.

At 6:00 a.m. on September 8, 1969, Srs. Berta and Corita, still wearing their flannel pajamas, opened the convent doors at 3121 Paseo to four-year-old Honora and her three-month-old brother, Hubert Rice. Their mother hugged them goodbye and left for her job as a nurse. Dana Brown followed. There were four babies and six preschoolers on the first day.

The start date of St. Vincent's Childcare Center coincided with some other notable events in history. On the same day in 1504, Michelangelo unveiled his *David* in Florence; the American Pledge of Allegiance was first recited in 1892; 3M began marketing Scotch transparent tape in 1930; and German forces began the Siege of Leningrad in 1941.

The sisters would have as notable an effect on the lives of the families they served, especially considering their lack of expertise and resources.

A LICENSE TO CARE?

The nuns knew nothing about running a childcare center or a business of any kind.

"Father Jim Lawbaugh had to give us money from his pocket to pay the first bill," Sr. Berta says.

The sisters often learned the ropes by getting caught in them. Their first lesson was in licensing. On a crisp, fall day a couple of months after opening, a woman showed up at the door and said, "I'm from licensing. I need to see your license."

"License?" said Sr. Berta. "You need a license to take care of toddlers?"

"It's illegal to have children under two in group care in the state of Missouri without a license," said the woman from the Missouri Division of Welfare.

"It is?"

"We could make an exception if a recognized religious institution runs the center."

"Does being Catholic count?"

It did.

"Our Catholic affiliation got the Missouri Division of Welfare to recognize what was one of the first childcare centers based outside a home in Kansas City," Sr. Berta says.

Although the sisters used their status as nuns to get a license for children two and under, they did not inform their BVM order that they had gone into the daycare business.

"Our community would have closed it if they'd known it was here," Sr. Berta says. "But they were in Dubuque, Iowa, and we were here. Nobody ever asked us, and we followed a 'don't ask, don't tell' policy."

Word may not have reached Iowa, but it soon spread through the east-side neighborhood, and more mothers began bringing their children. The sisters were able to hire more minders as the demand grew. The pay was minimum wage, $1.15 an hour. Sr. Corita says:

We hired Anna Jennings to direct the daycare. She would arrive at 7:00 a.m. and cook big breakfasts of pancakes, eggs, bacon, and sausages for the kids and the school staff. Miss Jennings was a good cook. She made it seem easy.

The childcare center soon had a dozen employees, although neither Sr. Berta nor Sr. Corita took a salary, and the cook also served the school students.

As enrollment grew, so did regulations. Letters from the Missouri Division of Welfare suggested the sisters often pushed the boundaries of them. One letter dated December 14, 1973, explains that the center must provide "35 square feet of floor space per child. Floor space occupied by permanent, built-in cabinets and shelves may not be considered as floor space available for play."

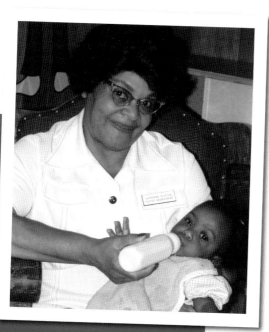

Catherine Gleaton

The state calculated the 1,446 square feet of available space was enough for 41 children.

If the state was suspicious of the venture, the church was downright opposed.

"Whoever heard of a church running a daycare?" sniffed Father Norman Rotert, a priest at the diocese. He implied that the bishop did not look favorably upon the center either.

Middle- and upper-class people didn't need childcare at the time because most moms stayed home. However, a second income was becoming more of a necessity to those living below the poverty line, and the number of single mothers struggling to take care of their kids was rising.

As each challenge appeared, the sisters started looking for a way to overcome it, taxing the limits of creativity as well as the law.

MOTHER'S LITTLE HELPERS

Sr. Berta got up every morning at 4:00 a.m. to make bread for the children. Then she and Sr. Corita welcomed the children who arrived for daycare around 7:00 a.m. and headed next door to St. Vincent Academy to assume their duties as principal and teacher.

Sr. Corita hired two people to watch over the daycare kids. Anna Jennings looked after the preschool-age kids during the day. The kids called her Grandma and crawled all over her like she was a boulder. Catherine Gleaton looked after the babies.

After school, the nuns stayed with the kids until six in the evening, when the parents picked them up.

At night, Srs. Berta and Corita painted classrooms, patched plaster, and cooked up ways to keep the kids comfortable and entertained. What made their schedule possible was an over-the-counter medication they bought at a drugstore nearby on Prospect.

Anna Jennings

The Comprehensive
Drug Abuse Prevention
and Control Act
restricted the use of
Black Beauties in 1971

*If Sr. Berta can't find a
solution, then one doesn't
exist.*

—Chris Sill-Rogers,
retired judge

Black Beauties (also known as Black Birds, Black Bombers, or Mother's Little Helpers)—a combination of amphetamine (speed) and dextroamphetamine (active salt in Adderall)—were widely available over the counter. They kept combat duty soldiers alert, truck drivers awake, housewives slim and trim, and they gave two nuns the energy to work night and day. Their side effects—mild to moderate euphoria, increased hyperactivity, increased awareness of surroundings, increased interest in normally boring activities, decreased appetite, and insomnia—were just what the sisters needed to keep their operation going.

They were willing to do whatever it took to make their charges happy, and sometimes their methods were as unorthodox as their tactics.

BABIES ON ICE

The Indian summer of 1969 resulted in some fussy babies who didn't like the heat. Anna Jennings complained to Sr. Berta, who put her creativity to quick use. She bought tubs used to feed cattle and installed them in the convent, where she filled them with ice. Then she positioned the fans to blow over the top. Presto! The whir of the fans and the cool breeze put the babies to sleep.

As the childcare enrollment grew, the remaining nuns moved into one room to make more space for the kids. Then Srs. Berta and Corita tore up the chapel in the convent to bring in even more children. Sr. Corita says:

That just horrified everybody, but more moms needed our service. The convent had two floors. As we got bigger, we wanted to put preschoolers on the second floor. The licensing department said we had to enclose the open stairwell. We wrote Hallmark a letter and asked for a small grant to enclose the stairwell, and J.E. Dunn sent a team to construct it.

The sisters built a playground with help from the teachers

When priests moved out of St. Vincent's rectory at 3110 Flora, the sisters saw it as an opportunity and moved the infants into the space so they could take care of more preschoolers in the convent.

The sisters deployed the same strategies at the childcare center as they did at the school. An early schedule for the center was as follows:

6:00 a.m.	Center opens
6:00-9:00 a.m.	Free play, group games, or TV. Breakfast is served during this time. Outdoor play if weather allows.
9:00 a.m.-12:00 p.m.	Education program. All learning areas are open, children move in areas according to interests and needs. Areas are math readiness, reading readiness, science, art, and motor development. A snack is served.
12:00-12:30 p.m.	Lunch
12:30-3:00 p.m.	Nap
3:00-6:00 p.m.	Free play, group activities, TV, or motor activities. Learning areas are sometimes open for part of this time. A snack is served. Outdoor play if weather permits.

St. Vincent's Rectory became a daycare

Oscar Huber later moved to Dallas and was the priest who administered last rites to President John F. Kennedy in 1963.

A HOME FOR THE LEFT BEHIND

The convent was still crowded with kids, with many more on a waiting list, so when a nine-room, brick-and-frame home at 3117 Paseo became available, Srs. Berta and Corita moved into it. A prior owner had painted it pink, so it soon became known as the Pink House. Sr. Berta says:

We spent summers when school was out remodeling it. One day, we were steaming the wallpaper off the house interior and set the steam pan in the open window. Someone called the fire department, thinking the house was on fire. We didn't have a refrigerator for months after we moved in because we couldn't afford one. We used to do the dishes in the bathtub because we didn't have a working kitchen sink.

Sr. Corita's mother came to visit when we were fixing up the house. She watched us sanding and repainting.

"I sent you to college so you'd never have to work like this," she said.

The sisters didn't mind the work, though, especially since the four-bedroom home gave them space to fill. Soon, daycare kids would find their way to the Pink House.

At the end of each day, most mothers welcomed their children with open arms when they picked them up after work. Darlene was a notable exception. Sr. Berta says:

A different person seemed to come every night to pick up her kids, Tony and Dorothy. It was rarely their mother, Darlene. Every night about six o'clock, the two siblings would start asking, "Who's going to take us home tonight?" We felt sorry for them because they never knew.

We started taking Tony and Dorothy home to the convent at night, thinking it would be a short-term thing. Others followed.

Between the rectory and the home was a big backyard, so we decided to make a playground for the kids and let them enjoy meals outside when the weather was good. We had to rent a jackhammer to break up some concrete, and it was quite a challenge to operate. Our religious education didn't prepare us to operate heavy machinery or build playgrounds, so our improvements didn't always work.

We put out picnic tables with benches for the toddlers. When we set them on the benches, every kid promptly slid to the ground. We really didn't know what we were doing. We learned things by doing them wrong.

CARE UP, CHURCH DOWN

While the sisters expanded their services, the Vincentian fathers running St. Vincent's worked on an exit plan. As early as 1948, Pastor Oscar Huber had written in church bulletins about declining membership.

When St. Vincent's was built in the 1920s, the diocese presumed the neighborhood would mushroom. Instead, the population shrank, and donations declined. The parish was supposed to send a portion of the collection plate to support the diocese. Instead, in the 1960s, it began borrowing money from the diocese. School enrollment had slipped below 100, the point where the diocese would shut it down.

Father John Sharpe was making arrangements with the Diocese of Kansas City-Saint Joseph to turn over the church property. He called Sr. Corita to his office to tell her the fathers would not support the school or the daycare.

The fate of their operation would soon be in the hands of the diocese.

"Given what the bishop thinks of nuns running childcare centers, we are in big trouble," Sr. Berta said to her friend that night.

"Should we just quit this?" was the response. "We can't be a further burden to the diocese, and we don't have the money to run this place either."

Sr. Berta's eyes darted sideways then narrowed as a crooked smile crept across her face.

"Oh, dear," said Sr. Corita, suspecting calamity around the bend.

Left to right: Nickie Collins, Harry Patterson, and Michael Gillis

CHAPTER 6

FLOWER CHILDREN IN THE ATTIC

Hippies like Peter Sandwall
proved popular teachers

"Berta, *Berta*, you forgot to turn in the surplus form, and now the food won't be here in time," said Sr. Corita, from her office in what had once been the school's chapel.

In 1968, the United States Congress established the Child Care Food Program for children in qualified childcare programs to get surplus foods from the U.S. Department of Agriculture. The sisters went through a detailed application that involved filling out dozens of forms.

"Corita, look at your desk. It's right in front of you," Sr. Berta snapped from her own desk, set up just outside.

"Berta, don't you think I looked before I started yelling at you?"

Sr. Berta emitted a sigh of impatience as she got up and, muttering under her breath, began riffling through the papers piled on Sr. Corita's desk.

With the zeal of a prizefighter brandishing a trophy, she held up the requisition form. "See, Corita, *see*, here it is."

"That's not the one I need," responded Corita.

Sr. Berta shook her head with a smile on her face. They both laughed as they headed down to the railway tracks to pick up the surplus food off a train car. Today, the agent handed them four bags of bulgur.

"What's bulgur?" Sr. Berta asked. "And what in the world are we supposed to do with it?"

"We have more important problems than figuring out how to cook bulgur," Sr. Corita reminded her. "Let's drop this off and hit the road."

As was their custom when they needed to think, the sisters took a road trip. Today, they headed for Des Moines, Iowa, to visit Sr. Corita's family.

The getaway car

Confinement in their white, 1961 Rambler station wagon was the only way they could escape the hive of interruptions. The placid, plains scenery around the newly built Interstate 35 relaxed them.

CHANGING OF THE GUARD

Changes at the parish kept the two so engaged in conversation that Sr. Berta failed to make any of her usual wisecracks to Sr. Corita, who was driving, about the billboards they passed.

Father Lawbaugh, a staunch ally of the school, would soon be leaving.

"The diocese isn't supporting the school at all," he had told the nuns. "Even with collections, fundraising, and donations, we are barely making ends meet."

He had struck up a friendship with a social worker at St. Vincent's, Sandra Claudell, and his vow of celibacy was proving impossible to keep. The two decided to do lay ministry work in Lawrence, Massachusetts.

Just before the 1969 school year started, Father Lawbaugh left with Sandra in her father's two-tone Chevrolet Impala. They wound up in Boston and married a couple months later at City Hall. In the parish bulletin of September 21, 1969, Pastor Sharpe wrote:

Father Lawbaugh has requested me to ask you not to think so much of the pain you may feel in his leaving St. Vincent's as of the love you shared with him when he served the family of God here.

He has decided to engage in an experimental type of apostolate elsewhere and asks our prayers for his success.

Personally, I regret his leaving the parish. I have been amazed at the multitude of activities in which he was engaged. I feel so much in need of his advice, encouragement and assistance. Bereft of them, I turn—all the more in need—to you…

To listen to the sisters, you would think they have a tumultuous relationship, but their love is so deep, so kind, so enduring. They are true life partners.

—**Susie Roling, former employee**

Throughout my life, I have kept the feelings of love in those few years as a priest.

—**Father James Lawbaugh, former St. Vincent's pastor who became a Mormon**

The departure of the head pastor, Reverend James Cashman, soon after that fueled rumors about the future of St. Vincent's.

"The diocese is going to close St. Vincent's school. I know it," said Sr. Berta.

"Oh, Berta, we have to have faith," said Sr. Corita. "The kids are so happy and loving; the parents are so happy and hard working. Our school has to be blessed. Maybe there will be a miracle."

"Just in case we don't get one, let's lay out our options," said Sr. Berta. They both concluded they weren't prepared to leave the sisterhood. "We could ask the BVMs to assign us to a school somewhere else. We could look for teaching jobs around Kansas City on our own, or we could fight the bishop if he closes us down."

"We need to be realistic. We can't defy the diocese; we have to follow the rules," Sr. Corita replied. "Besides, we have nothing."

"Hey, you conned me into coming to St. Vincent's," Sr. Berta said. "Now that I'm here, I'm not giving this up without a fight."

An army of aides would soon appear from a most unexpected source: The Ecstatic Umbrella.

PLAN H, FOR HIPPIES

The Ecstatic Umbrella was a cooperative in midtown Kansas City, first at 3800 McGee, then at 3621 Charlotte. It operated a free health clinic, daycare, and a food co-op. It was a magnet for young people, both those in trouble and those seeking to

ST. VINCENT
SCHOOL
1968-1969
BOOKER T. WASHINGTON ROOM

save the world. Young homosexual kids whose parents had thrown them out came for counseling. Drug users took their stashes to the center's lab, which analyzed chemicals to keep kids from bad trips. An article in *The Kansas City Times* published October 31, 1969, reported the lab had recently determined that a substance local drug dealers peddled as LSD was actually a tranquilizer for elephants.

Tamara Chaves and Peter Sandwall arrived in the fall of 1969.

Tamara Chaves grew up in a wealthy New Jersey family of Bolivian origin. She attended boarding schools and lived in a sheltered, conservative environment. She wanted to be a beautician, but her parents wanted her to be a doctor or a lawyer. She defied them and moved to New York City, where she soon met Peter Sandwall, a tall young man with flowing, dark-brown locks and a thick beard. He was everything Chaves's straitlaced parents had warned her to avoid. She says:

Peter was the ultimate hippie-artist. He was a pied piper who made friends with everyone. He painted and did etchings. Peter went to Woodstock, and a photographer captured him naked in a photo that appeared in Life magazine. After he came back from Woodstock, we made a decision to hitchhike across the country. We ran low on money in Kansas City.

They told a staff member at The Ecstatic Umbrella that they needed jobs and a place to stay.

"I know these two nuns," he said. "The diocese is threatening to cut their funding. They need help."

Sr. Berta describes her first meeting with the couple:

Peter looked like Jesus Christ with his long hair and beard. He said he was an artist, so Corita asked him to teach an art class. Tamara, who had such a melting smile, could speak Spanish and sew, so we told her we would add those subjects to our curriculum if she would teach them. We offered them each $50 a week, plus room and board in the attic.

We believed that if you were a loving, kind person, you could be a teacher. We didn't say, 'What degree do you have?' We asked, 'What energy do you have?

—**Sr. Corita**

The Pink House at 3117 Paseo had a finished attic, which they turned into a dormitory for flower children. In return, their houseguests helped out by teaching classes and working in the childcare center. Word got out that men who opposed the Vietnam War could fulfill the community service requirement to become conscientious objectors by working at St. Vincent's.

Soon, the attic was crowded with young men and a few women who accompanied them. The young hippies were so hooked on the mission that they recruited others from their network of young people who were committed to solving societal problems.

They each taught subjects that interested them. Blue jeans replaced habits. Most did not have teaching certificates, but the students were crazy about them.

The flower children brought more than just energy and new ideas, though.

POT AND PASSION

Tamara's 16-year-old brother, Carlos Chaves, showed up next. He wasn't much of a student back in New Jersey, and was spending more time in the principal's office than in the classroom. After a blowout with his parents in 1970, he came to visit his sister.

Carlos hung out with the group at the Pink House, where he played board games like Yahtzee. Sr. Berta noticed how good he was at math and asked him to tutor students.

His friend, Chuck Mercuri, came to Kansas City with him. Mercuri happened to be an excellent mechanic, a skill that Sr. Berta would soon put to use. No talent went to waste around St. Vincent's.

Tamara and Peter wanted more privacy than the dormitory provided. They convinced the Carpenters Union to let them serve as the caretakers at Carpenters

The sisters moved to the Pink House to make room for more children in the convent

Hall, a social club for the members of the union, at 3114 Paseo. There, they started having parties, dubbed Peter's Feasts. Tamara says:

One summer night, we invited everyone from St. Vincent's, The Ecstatic Umbrella, and the free health clinic, and we threw a giant party. I cooked a big pig. We were on the top floor, and we blasted music all over the hall. On the playlist were "Crystal Blue Persuasion" (Tommy James and The Shondells), "My Cherie Amour" (Stevie Wonder), "Spinning Wheel" (Blood, Sweat and Tears), and "Bad Moon Rising" (Creedence Clearwater Revival).

Carlos Chaves bought a 1963 Buick Special station wagon. He and Peter liked to cruise around the area. One day, they were in the West Bottoms and spotted patches of hemp growing around a drainage ditch. Carlos says:

In the 1950s, the government was hybridizing hemp to strengthen it for rope and clothing. It is in the marijuana family but has a lower THC content—but it was free. We loaded it into my station wagon, which we left parked in front of the hall.

The next morning, the sisters passed by the car and thought they saw Peter and Tamara in sleeping bags. Sr. Berta says:

I knocked on the window to wake them up because the kids were coming. The sleeping bags turned out to be what looked like bags of marijuana. We quickly walked away. Later that morning, I saw Carlos bringing in pillowcases of the stuff. I asked him what he was doing, and he said he was going to dry hemp in the clothes dryer.

I told him that wasn't such a good idea. When I told Corita, she said, "These are the true flower children. They are all very good people, even if they don't always do the right thing."

Hippies brought hemp harvest to St. Vincent's

AN ARMY IN THE ATTIC

Peter and Tammy liked to hang out at The Levee, a bar in a historic, red-brick building at 16 West 43rd Street. Soon after its opening in 1965, the place became a counterculture hotspot. Occasionally, Srs. Berta and Corita would join them.

The foursome tended to attract the attention of the young hippies and idealists who frequented the place, and often Peter invited them back to the Pink House. By 1971, there were about two dozen young idealists, conscientious objectors, and flower children from around the country at St. Vincent's. They brought new skills, ideas about community activism, and a determination to change the world.

Not all the faculty wore torn blue jeans and granny dresses, though. Helen Gragg, a stocky, five-foot-tall dynamo who had gone to St. Vincent's as a student, taught reading and typing and dressed primly in skirts. On the second floor, she held court over a room full of big, iron, manual typewriters and the reluctant typists who sat in front of them.

"We wore our poor little fingers out on those machines," Kim Randolph says. "Mrs. Gragg could type more than 100 words a minute, and she was determined to make sure we could too." She glared at the children with her black, Irish eyes and managed to keep her class in line.

Helen, who was quite conservative, had never owned a pair of pants before the sisters came to St. Vincent's. They insisted she buy a pair so she could accompany them on a trip to the Ozarks with some of the students. She may have been straitlaced, but she shared a love of teaching with the young activists, so they all plodded and plotted together. They made for a ragtag army that was no more obedient than their two sister generals.

In the evenings, the gang hung out at the Pink House and talked about what to do.

"Can you believe the Vincentians are giving up on this place?" Sr. Berta told a crowd of a dozen huddled around their living room coffee table. The group included Rich Koch, Claudia York, Peter Sandwall, Tamara Chaves, and Chuck Chaves. She told them about the plan to hand St. Vincent's over to the diocese.

Helen Gragg

The difference between Corita and me is she doesn't worry about anything, and I worry about everything.

—Sr. Berta

The sisters do things and hope the money comes later.

—Claudia York, former teacher

Corita avoided the limelight. She learned to do payroll and human resources. I worked on fundraising and communications. We are a good pair.

—Sr. Berta

"The bishop really wants us out," she continued, taking a sip from the Budweiser she liked to drink after she mowed the grass. "The diocese will shut us down without a second thought."

"I see the effects of what we do every day," said Claudia York, who had taken a job at St. Martin's Center but had moved back into the convent in March 1971. "In four or five months, a child who wouldn't speak at all is now talking in full sentences. We cannot let that go."

A chorus of lamentations followed. Then Sr. Corita spoke in a voice made raspy by her ever-present cigarettes. "Well, now, we don't know for sure what the diocese will do. Things will work out. You'll see," she said, sipping from a scotch on the rocks.

"We have to make a plan in case this happens," Rich said.

"A plan would be a novel idea," Sr. Berta wisecracked. Then she followed her joke with a flurry of ideas:

Maybe we should write the pope. We could buy the building and run the school ourselves. We could ask the Vincentian fathers if they would let us stay here for free. Maybe someone at Legal Aid could help. Let's make sure the neighborhood knows about this. When the diocese finds out how much our parents love the school and daycare, it will make it harder for them to close the doors. Let's start staging protests. Maybe we could get the kids involved.

Sr. Berta possessed an uncanny ability to mobilize those around her and had more marketing savvy than many on Madison Avenue. Peter promised the next art class would involve making protest posters. Claudia promised to look for grants and call organizations to see if they would contribute to the school.

The sisters stayed up until 3:00 a.m. plotting a campaign. Then they got up at 6:00 a.m. ready to execute it. Sleep was often the first luxury they cast aside.

The next morning, the two went to see Father Sharpe. "The Vincentians are giving up the church," he told them. "So we will not stand in their way." He cautioned that they would need the bishop's approval to keep the operation going.

Sr. Corita during a voter drive

PINT-SIZED PROTESTERS LEARN FROM PANTHERS

Because Kim Randolph's mom dropped her off at 6:00 a.m. and didn't pick her up until 6:00 p.m., she spent a lot of time with the sisters and kept her ears open:

The sisters never had secrets. I heard about how the diocese wasn't making money at St. Vincent's. Tuition was on a sliding scale, and few of the parents were paying full fare. There were more kids and not enough money. I was worried that the school would close and ready to help fight to keep it open. I volunteered to organize a protest.

In art class the next day, we made signs out of construction paper and tempera paint that said, "Save Our School" and "Keep St. Vincent's."

After school that day, as many as 50 children flew out the front door as if shot by a cannon. Holding their signs as high as they could, they marched up 31st Street to Paseo, south to Linwood, then east to Flora. Periodically, they swatted each other with their signs, and they got the attention of thousands of passing motorists. But their territory was only one square block.

Sr. Berta wanted to cover all the bases. The Black Panthers were known for their skill at community organizing. She learned they would be speaking at the downtown campus of Park College and thought her students might find it educational. She says:

I got the bright idea to take the seventh and eighth graders. I wanted them to see different points of view. On the stage were nine black guys wearing black leather jackets and berets pitched at a rakish angle. They were all bearing rifles and yelling, "Death to the white devil!"

I looked around and realized I was the only white devil in the room!

The speakers called for overthrowing capitalism and replacing it with a "dictatorship of the proletariat." One warned of "CIA informers" and "pig police" in the audi-

ence who could "go to hell or wait until we put them there." The speakers all cursed like sailors. I hissed at the children, "Don't listen!"

Every time the kids heard a curse word, they covered it up with a loud "Uuhhhmm," and I kept trying to shut them up. I didn't want to draw any more attention to us.

Then I started worrying about what was going to happen when the diocese found out I'd taken a group of middle schoolers to an event where every fourth word was an obscenity.

She would soon find out when the two determined sisters became one more headache for the bishop.

Students were always ready to protest

Students, many of whom had never left Kansas City, got treated to vacations like this one to Colorado

CHAPTER 7
SIEGE OF ST. VINCENT'S

St. Vincent students and their parents beg the bishop to keep the school open

Bishop Charles Herman Helmsing had a meeting one day in 1971 that was sure to add to his tribulations.

Pope John XXIII had nominated the Shrewsbury, Missouri, native to oversee the Diocese of Kansas City-Saint Joseph in 1962. After taking part in all four sessions of the Second Vatican Council, he came to Kansas City to implement its decrees among the estimated 140,000 Catholics in the diocese.

Instead, he found himself mired in local struggles. According to *The History of the Diocese of Kansas City-St. Joseph*, by Kevin Kelly, "Perhaps no bishop in the history of the diocese had more challenges before him than Bishop Helmsing."

Civil rights clashes and the Vietnam War pitted black against white and young against old. These divisive issues played out in the Catholic Church, which was undergoing its own revolution. On November 22, 1963—the same day Lee Harvey Oswald assassinated President John F. Kennedy—the Second Vatican Council voted to celebrate Mass in vernacular languages instead of Latin. Priests were to face their flocks to celebrate it. According to Kelly's book:

All these changes required a massive education effort on top of expensive architectural changes to churches at a time when Bishop Helmsing and the Diocese of Kansas City-St. Joseph could ill afford them.

The Council caused an identity crisis among both the clergy and women and men religious as it called for expanding the role of the laity. Many would leave their religious vocations at a time when fewer young people were hearing the call to religious life.

From 1965 to 1970, the number of women religious serving the diocese declined from just more than 1,200 to slightly less than 1,000…During the 1970s, some 45 diocesan priests also resigned and many of them subsequently married.

As priests and nuns left their orders, migration changed the demographics among the diocese's 98 parishes and missions that covered 15,000 square miles and 27 counties in northwestern Missouri. The riots that followed the assassination of Martin Luther King, Jr. on April 4, 1968, accelerated white flight to the suburbs. Many parishes found themselves with less than a third of the pews filled—and the collection plate take shrank accordingly.

While the inner cities emptied, the diocese was in the midst of a building boom to erect churches to serve the suburbs sprouting like kudzu across the metro. From 1963 to 1965, the diocese established seven new parishes in suburban areas. The diocese spent almost $30 million in construction from the late 1950s to 1965. By 1962, the diocese was about $10 million in debt, according to *The History of the Diocese of Kansas City-St. Joseph.* Bishop Helmsing had to borrow $1 million just to meet the interest payments on the outstanding debt.

Something had to give.

CONSOLIDATE TO CONQUER

The Diocesan Council, under the direction of Bishop Charles Helmsing, planned to merge three of the poorest parochial schools on the city's east side: St. Vincent's, Holy Name, and Annunciation. Pastors and principals in these parishes were struggling. The collection plates couldn't support the massive buildings with aging boilers and flaking pipes.

According to *The Catholic Key* (*catholickey.org*), "In the early 1970s, Holy Name's parish council began discussions with St. Vincent's and Annunciation parishes about consolidation."

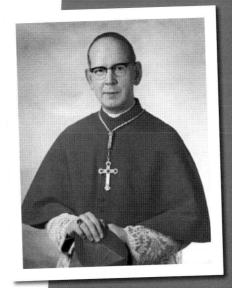

Bishop Charles Helmsing headed the Diocese of Kansas City-Saint Joseph

A series of meetings to negotiate the particulars took place. For five hours on April 7, 1971, parishioners and area residents debated this idea at a meeting held at Annunciation, 2800 Linwood Blvd., according to an article in *The Kansas City Times* dated April 10, 1971. It explained, "The main point of disagreement was which two buildings should be for the consolidated school and which building should be put to an optional use."

A planning committee made up of four representatives from each church—the pastor, a faculty member, and two parents—would make the decision. The committee would then select a principal and develop a curriculum based on what worked best between the three schools.

The financial situation and building repairs on the to-do list did not bode well for St. Vincent's. Since 1962, the parish had been drawing on its surplus funds to pay ordinary expenses, according to *This Far By Faith*, by Charles M. Coleman. In 1967, the parish made $31,358 worth of repairs, but many more were needed. This exhausted the surplus, and the parish started borrowing money on a monthly basis to meet expenses. By 1971, the debt was an estimated $50,000.

Within a couple of months of the contentious meeting, the diocese announced that it would merge the three schools into the Father Benedict Justice School with two campuses: Holy Name and Annunciation.

St. Vincent's was to disappear entirely from the diocese's parochial school network.

That must have provided some satisfaction to Bishop Helmsing. Rumors had been flying about what was going on at the parish for a couple of years. He had heard that the nuns were teaching classrooms full of Baptists, consorting with hippies, and had men living in the convent. Reports of wild parties with rock and roll music made their way to the chancery.

Bishop Helmsing would brook no interference from liberal Catholics. Soon after he came to Kansas City, he launched a campaign against the *National Catholic Reporter (NCR)* for its policy of "crusading against the Church's teachings." Helmsing took issue with the paper's stance on birth control, priestly celibacy, and criticism of the hierarchy. He demanded the weekly newspaper remove the word *Catholic* from its name.

On this particular day, Bishop Helmsing was about to do something similar to St. Vincent's—strip it of its affiliation with the diocese. Minutes before he was to meet with the two nuns, he heard several people chattering outside his office. They didn't sound happy…or docile.

Parents and teachers began plotting
how to fight the bishop

NUNS VERSUS THE BISHOP

When Sr. Berta first learned of the consolidation plans, she gathered the inner circle of parents, staff, and volunteers at the Pink House. Over a dinner of soup and bologna sandwiches, Sr. Berta told them:

The diocese doesn't think we should be providing daycare as a part of our services. The bishop doesn't like it that we have more Baptists in the school than Catholics. And he has accused us of being rabble rousers. He is going to shut us down.

This is where the road blows up and we blaze a new trail. If we go out on our own, we won't have to jump through all these hoops—hoops that make no sense. Let's get a thousand people to storm the diocese offices.

Sr. Corita tried to calm her down.

"Now, Berta, let's look at this from the diocese's perspective," she said. "We are a threat to them, even if we don't mean to be. We have to proceed with caution."

"I'm going to request a meeting with the bishop," Sr. Berta said. Sr. Corita looked doubtful but knew it would be pointless to get in her friend's way.

The next day, Sr. Corita sent out an interoffice memo to faculty to discuss how to approach the bishop. It read: "Good Morning, All! A reminder—God Willing—Faculty meeting will be tonight after school—3:15. See you there."

At the appointed time in the summer of 1971, the two sisters—with Claudia York, Rich Koch, and board president and mother of four students Anita Bradford—marched up the steps of the Catholic Chancery at 300 East 36th Street. Once the private home of William McGraw Reid, a prominent Kansas Citian, the building was an imposing, Elizabethan manor.

"Hmm. Wonder how much this cost?" Sr. Berta said. "We could keep St. Vincent's going at least 10 years with the money."

We had one common goal. We wanted these kids to have what they deserved—a good school and a safe place to grow up.

—Tamara Chaves Cicogna, former teacher

The rest of the group was too busy rehearsing their arguments to pay any attention to the architecture. They discussed whether to call the news stations if the bishop turned them down.

"Father Norman Rotert talked to us before the meeting and gave us hope that things might be okay," Claudia says. "But I think he was just trying to calm us down to keep us from calling the press."

In Bishop Helmsing's office, Claudia began, "The other schools want to go back to traditional teaching. Our parents don't want to go backwards." She told him how engaged the children were in learning.

Sr. Corita told him:

Our school has to be blessed. It has to be. When the public schools can't handle kids, they send them to us. We've taken children who were thrown out of public schools, who have learning problems, who might not get an education without St. Vincent's. We took in a big, tall kid who used to dig graves at night. He had broken a desk over a teacher's head in public school. He has become our star basketball player. He is now the sweetest, most gentle soul. What will happen to these children if St. Vincent's goes away?

Claudia described how the diocese worked in her hometown:

I come from an area in Kentucky that is 70 percent Catholic and is in the richest parish in town. We have to share our money with poorer parishes. We keep those parishes open by making richer ones share. You have all these higher-income parishes in southern Kansas City. Why don't they share?

The bishop pointed out that most of the families at St. Vincent's were Baptist, not Catholic. "Why should we keep this church open?" he said. "No one is even going to Mass."

"They are going to school," Sr. Berta replied. "Caring for the preschool kids allows women to work, which is keeping families above water. Closing the school and the daycare would irretrievably rend the fabric of the neighborhood."

"We are here for the children," Sr. Corita added. "The children deserve the best. The best is love. That's what we are trying to do for them."

The bishop told Srs. Berta and Corita that if they would just leave town, the parents would give up, and the consolidation would move forward smoothly.

"You're a hypocrite," said Rich. "We are having great luck with St. Vincent's, and you are going to close us down."

The bishop threatened to kick him out of the meeting.

"If we leave this corner, these children will be lost," Sr. Corita said. "They will have nothing. There is just no other school like ours in the city."

Their pleas didn't move the bishop, who warned them that they could not stop the consolidation.

While the rest of the group buzzed with outrage, Sr. Corita was quiet. She was usually the one who assured others that something good would surely come out of this.

OUT OF ORDER

The BVM Order in Dubuque, Iowa, had been hearing about the goings on down south at St. Vincent's. Among the reports was a rumor about two sisters consorting with men who lived in their convent. Sr. Berta says: The mother general called us one night, and Rich answered the phone. When I got on the phone, she said she was going to send a delegation to Kansas City for a visitation.

"Are you dating these men?" she asked me, point-blank.

"Get a life," I told her. "If I were going to date, it wouldn't be some scraggly haired hippie who needs a bath. It would be a man with some money."

When the order threatened to throw us out, I said, "Go ahead."

She put down the phone and complained, "The BVMs are more worried about whether we are dating than what we are doing."

Threats from the motherhouse were wasted on Sr. Berta. Belonging to the order fell far down on her priority list. Keeping the school and child-care programs going took all the energy she had.

The incident did prompt the sisters to make a rule that men couldn't answer the phone in the future. And when the head nuns came for a visit several months later, the sisters asked the men to find another place to stay for a few days.

That was as far as the sisters were willing to go against the male teachers who were having such a beneficial effect on the students.

Catholic Chancery at
300 East 36th Street

COACH KOCH

The sports teams—basketball, track, and volleyball—at St. Vincent's had a reputation for losing. St. Vincent's competed against Bishop Miege, Holy Name, Redemptorist, St. James, and St. Theresa's. Kim Randolph, who was on the track team, says:

We didn't have a nice track or a nice sandpit. We didn't have uniforms, equipment, or even shoes in many cases. I did the long jump barefoot and once landed on a bottle. An ambulance took me to St. Luke's Hospital. We were ragtag.

Mister Rich took our track team to the next level. He gave us a winner instinct. He told us: "Our opponents could laugh at us, put us down. We aren't going to have fancy tennis shoes or better training facilities. The best way to make them shut up is to beat them."

And that's what we did. We beat them every year until the league made us put on tennis shoes.

The basketball team wasn't as fortunate. Its first year, the St. Vincent's team lost every game, but that didn't dampen team spirit. According to Coach Koch:

The highlight of the season was playing against the Guardian Angels' team. They were down 48-0 when a St. Vincent's player nailed a half-court shot at the buzzer…into the opponents' basket. His teammates carried him off the court cheering like they'd won an NBA title!

The real challenge facing the school wasn't basketball; it was the bishop.

St. Vincent's volleyball team

THE BISHOP SQUEEZE PLAY

Rumors swirled that a shutdown of the school was imminent. On August 28, 1971, Claudia wrote in her diary, "The world is falling apart." It would become official three days later.

On August 31, 1971, the head pastor of St. Vincent's, Father John Sharpe, sent a letter to Sr. Corita notifying her that St. Vincent's school no longer existed. The letter threatened that, if the sisters continued to operate the school, it would be without the blessing or financial support of the parish, the Vincentian order, or the diocese.

A letter from Bishop Helmsing followed shortly, on September 3. It made clear that the diocese would not include St. Vincent's in its parochial school system and would "no longer bear any responsibility for what happens to the school."

Sr. Corita, who hadn't seemed herself in the weeks following the bishop's meeting, summoned Sr. Berta and read her the letter. She put it down on her desk and announced with steely calm:

It's time to take off our habits and put on our boxing gloves. The children and their families are too important to give up on them. We can not desert them. We have to stick to our guns. We need to figure out a way to keep the school and childcare programs going. This is right in our hearts.

This letter seemed to turn Sr. Corita from a conservative peacemaker into a rabble rouser.

Sr. Berta beamed at her friend and suggested they make a case to keep the school going without diocesan support. Sr. Berta called Bishop Helmsing and invited him for a visit. Then she called a meeting of the inner circle—Claudia, Rich, Anita, Anna Jennings, Mattie Flanagan, and a couple of teachers—and told them to gird up for battle.

Berta was the one with the ideas, and Corita was the one who knew how to execute them.

—Claudia York, former teacher

Coach Rich Koch and the St. Vincent's basketball team

The most important lesson I learned from the sisters is to think with your heart.

—**Jonathon Sabel,
daycare alumnus and
current sales consultant**

You can't run a school on nothing, but we thought you could.

—**Sr. Corita**

Derek Collins

Claudia asked David Kierst, a Legal Aid attorney who represented the American Indian Association, housing rights, and the SAC-20, for help. He was well known as a community organizer. They strategized in the living room of the Pink House.

Sr. Berta imagined filling the huge, second-floor gymnasium, where St. Vincent families could show their support for keeping the school open. The bishop would be right up front, near the door.

"Oh no, you don't want to do that," said the boyfriend of one of the teachers. He worked as a convention planner. "You are trying to convince him to do something he doesn't want to do. You don't put him near the door. You want to crowd him so he feels defenseless. Put him in a corner with all the parents in front of him."

So that's exactly what they did.

On the day of Bishop Helmsing's visit, David pulled up at 3104 Flora in his 10-year-old, white Rambler American. A lot of people in the inner city knew the car. The kids also knew he would give them 50 cents to watch it. One little boy walked toward his car while a teenager approached from the other side. He heard the little one say, "That's my cracker. Leave him alone."

He smiled to himself as he entered the social hall in the basement and encountered more than 250 parents, teachers, and children. The bishop, one of a handful of white people in the room, was as far from the door as he could possibly be. People were taking the bishop to task, and the tone was heated.

"We don't want to consolidate," said one parent.

"Our inner-city children deserve a good education just as much as the rich kids in the suburbs," said another parent.

The bishop told the crowd, "My children, you don't understand."

"We aren't your children, and that's not the deal we want," Sr. Berta fired back. "We want to stay separate and independent. We'll raise our own money and keep the school open."

The bishop looked from side to side like he was planning an escape. Sr. Berta says:

He was afraid to tell us no, so he started suggesting conditions. He said we would have to pay rent to the diocese. We would have to sign a document saying the diocese would have no financial liability for our school. We could not even use the name St. Vincent's for the school or the childcare center.

"Do you have enough money to operate for a year?" he asked.

Sr. Berta assured him they had plenty of money for salaries and other expenses.

They had about $200 in the bank.

Renee Collins, Derek's sister, with Udell Walker (right), and unidentified St. Vincent's student

CHAPTER 8
FILL 'ER UP

Students sold candy bars to raise money for the school

"We aren't Catholic anymore. We are on our own," Sr. Corita announced over the school's intercom on the first day of school on September 14, 1971—the first day without diocese support. "That means no more plaid skirts. We're going to come up with a new uniform."

The uniforms were the easy part. Sr. Berta chose a polyester, burgundy tunic with matching pants. Sr. Corita chose a temporary name: The 31st Street Neighborhood School.

Without priests to oversee them, Mass, communion, and confession disappeared from the school. So, unfortunately, did funding.

Sr. Corita told the teachers they weren't going to get paid for a while. To underscore their changed circumstances, the diocese soon sent a directory that listed all the nuns at area churches and Catholic schools.

"We've been deleted," said Sr. Berta to Sr. Corita. They were both stooped over their bathtub, doing the dishes. The kitchen sink in the Pink House still didn't work. "Can you believe it?"

"Do you think we'll make it?" Sr. Berta asked. "Where are we going to get the money to keep our doors open?"

"Hand me a plate" was Sr. Corita's only response.

Everyone connected to the school formerly known as St. Vincent's would soon go through a crash course in fundraising as feeding the coffers became as important as feeding the chickens.

Top candy sellers won trips to the Ozarks

FROM HELL RAISERS TO FUNDRAISERS

Reading teacher Willie Mae Burke was driving the school's station wagon on a clear fall day in 1971. After classes, she dropped off Kim and 10 of her classmates in Mission Hills. They scattered in all directions. Kim stood in front of Ewing Kauffman's house at 5955 Mission Drive. The rambling, Spanish-style mansion looked like a fortress to her. She tried to remember what Sr. Berta often told the students.

"You have the ability to face any situation. You don't have to be ashamed about yourselves and where you live. You can go anywhere." She repeated this to herself like a mantra as she walked up the sidewalk that seemed about six blocks long.

The prospect of a trip to the Ozarks prompted Kim to ring the bell. The class that sold the most candy bars won the trip. Back at the school, strings for each class stretched down the central hall. On each hung a horse. After Sr. Corita announced the weekly fundraising totals for each class, Sr. Berta advanced the horses to show how much candy each class had sold.

"Would you like to buy some of our World's Finest chocolate bars?" Kim squeaked. "They are 50 cents a bar." The housekeeper who answered the door couldn't resist the pitch and bought an entire case of 24 bars. The candy sales brought in about $3,000 a year.

The parents also got involved in raising money.

In December, the parents had a party in one of the classrooms to report on their efforts. Anita Bradford, who was new in town, was among them. All four of her young children attended St. Vincent's school and loved it. She didn't have other options. Her husband's employer had transferred him from Denver to Kansas City, but the Kansas City office had refused to work with a black person. So, she took a job as a mail sorter for a direct-mail service. She reported to the group that also included several teachers:

Every extra penny went to enhance the school or open the door for another student.

—Kim Randolph, school alumna

I talked one of our suppliers, International Paper, into giving us a five-figure donation. At the company Christmas party at my boss's house, where we were drinking, I started asking people if they knew how we could get some money to help the school. The owners of the company wrote big checks too.

Bradford also talked about meeting the director of the Model Cities program, Jim Threatt.

According to the *Encyclopedia of American History: Postwar United States, 1946 to 1968,* (Revised Edition, vol. IX), "The Model Cities funded efforts to confront social and economic problems in poor, urban areas throughout the United States." Congress passed the program, which involved federal, state, and local resources, into law in 1966 under the aegis of the Department of Housing and Urban Development. It was part of President Lyndon B. Johnson's desire to conquer poverty and build a Great Society.

Cities went through a multi-phase planning process and submitted proposals for improvements. By 1968, HUD had selected 75 cities out of 200 that applied for planning grants. Kansas City was one of them.

Twenty percent of the funds were for education efforts. Bradford said Threatt promised to look into what he could do for The 31st Street Neighborhood School.

The group cheered her good news. According to Bradford:

Everyone was in a fine mood. One of the volunteers brought cookies and said she made them with marijuana. I was glad to hear it. Everyone got quiet and just ate their cookies. Then we put on some rhythm and blues music, and everyone danced.

Only a few blocks away, Srs. Berta and Corita and a few volunteers were playing poker at Anna Jennings's house, a gathering place for St. Vincent's families.

Claudia York reported that she had invited the new mayor, Charles Wheeler, for a tour. "He fell in love with the place and donated money out of his own pocket." He encouraged the city council to fund the school.

Tamara Chaves convinced the Hall Family Foundation to donate funds to start a Girl Scout troop, which she volunteered to run. It was the first, largest, and best-supplied all-black troop in the city.

Tamara's brother, Carlos Chaves, stuffed envelopes with flyers to blanket the neighborhood with requests for donations.

Claudia, Rich Koch, and Peter Sandwall wrote to every foundation in the United States they could find that issued grants for alternative schools. They sent out more than 100 letters.

"If people just knew what we were doing here, they would support us," Sr. Corita said, dealing the cards.

Kansas City Mayor Charles Wheeler became a great friend to St. Vincent's

NO BOOKS TO COOK

Rich came into the office one day and saw Berta opening envelopes with checks.

"We aren't an official nonprofit," Rich said. "We could get into trouble accepting these checks."

"David Kierst at Legal Aid could help," said Claudia, who was putting books back on shelves. David had been coming to St. Vincent events and was familiar with the school's mission. He had also incorporated more than two dozen nonprofits in the inner city.

David came and told them that converting to a nonprofit was a fairly straightforward process but that getting tax-exempt status was tougher.

"If you've never been in business, you can promise the IRS that you will be good, and the IRS can accept your promise," he said. "However, if you have been in business, you have to prove you've been good."

He cautioned the sisters about telling people that their donations were tax deductible when they did not have nonprofit status.

"I will need to go through your books to make sure they are in order," David said. "And I will need to see how you are documenting the donations."

The sisters looked sideways at each other and rolled their eyes.

"You do have books, don't you?" he asked.

"Couldn't you just make something up?" Sr. Berta suggested.

"You are asking me to do something I cannot do," David said. He told the sisters that to win nonprofit status they would need to have patience and structure—suspecting they had neither.

At that point, Berta handed $10 to one of the volunteers. "Go to the liquor store at 31st and Paseo with a box, lay it on the counter with the money, and tell them it's for the nuns." The store owner would fill up the box with some beer and scotch.

"I go to meetings at night all the time. I come back stone sober from everywhere except your place," David said to Sr. Berta.

There was a young law student working at Legal Aid, Michael Gunn, who was also a certified public accountant. David promised the sisters he would send Michael to help.

Michael showed up at the school office to help put together a set of books for The 31st Street Neighborhood School and Childcare Center. When he asked for records, Sr. Corita pointed him to a couple of cardboard boxes. They contained a jumble of receipts, bills, attendance sheets, and children's

The first thing out of Berta's mouth is usually a wild scheme.

—David Kierst, former Legal Aid attorney

This place should not be open today. We've done just about everything we could do to get ourselves shut down. Someone has looked out for us.

—Sr. Berta

Berta would take on the Lord, if the Lord got in the way.

—David Kierst

artwork. He poked into file drawers and spent a lot of time talking to Sr. Corita, trying to make sense of the often illegible pieces of paper.

"David, it can't be done," Michael reported after a few weeks. "I can set them up so they won't be in this chaos in the future, but I can't *recreate* a structure that didn't exist in the past."

"Your only hope is to piggyback on your association with the church," David told the sisters. He wondered how they had gotten grants from the city and funds from the Office of Equal Opportunity. He would soon find out.

On the day of their appointment with the IRS, the sisters put their scapular aprons over their black habits, donned their white wimples, and strung large strings of rosary beads at their waists. If they prayed, it was probably that the IRS not realize the diocese had severed its relationship with the school and with them. Michael carried in the boxes and the books he'd begun. He let the nuns talk about the children and the neighborhood.

After an hour, the IRS agent turned to the nuns and said, "Would you mind stepping out?"

Sitting in the anteroom outside, Sr. Berta whispered, "I hope the IRS agent doesn't see our tax records from last year." Sr. Corita had neglected to deduct Federal Insurance Contributions Act (FICA) taxes from the childcare employees, or to pay the employer portion. The law requires employers to pay half of the Social Security and Medicare contributions and deduct the other half from employees' wages.

FICA was as foreign to the sisters as Swahili. When Rich had explained it to them, they were horrified because they did not have the money to pay it. When they didn't respond to the initial letters, the IRS called and said an agent would pay them a visit.

Sr. Berta had padlocked the front door of the convent. "Shhh," she told the preschoolers. "We're going to play a game today. We're going to see how quiet we can be."

After rattling the chains for a few minutes, the agent had gone back to his office and, before his next visit, Sr. Corita had found the money to start paying the balance.

With the nuns out of earshot, the IRS agent whispered to Michael, "I'm granting them nonprofit status, but this will never happen again."

When the sisters told David the good news, he said, "Everyone who comes into contact with you gets sucked into your schemes. I shouldn't have been surprised that the IRS did too."

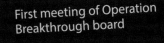

First meeting of Operation Breakthrough board

Getting the nuns incorporated and registered with Missouri wouldn't require a similar miracle, but it would require reining in Sr. Berta.

OPERATION BREAK THROUGH BREAKS THROUGH

"I have two requirements," David said. "You can't have a board bigger than nine people, and you have to have an accountant."

Sr. Berta promptly started handing out invitations like holy cards. *The more, the merrier* was her strategy. She invited parents of students, flower children volunteers, neighborhood activists, and, on occasion, someone she met on the street. Many agreed to participate. However, when David asked for a list of directors, she couldn't remember whom she had invited. She had neglected to write down their names. They would have to wait to see how many showed up for the first meeting.

One night at the Pink House, the sisters met with Rich, Claudia, and a few parents. They discussed possible names for the new organization. They couldn't keep The 31st Street Neighborhood School because they feared the diocese would evict them from the property. They wanted a name that would be portable if they had to move.

Someone suggested Operation Break Through. Sr. Berta latched on to it because she thought a name that sounded military would make it easier to get government money for the school's families.

David drew up the incorporation papers for Operation Break Through, which officially began on August 15, 1971. Its articles of incorporation stated: "The specific purpose of the corporation shall be to provide a program which meets the particular and peculiar educational needs of children."

Sr. Corita proposed a celebration. There was a seafood restaurant at 63rd and Troost called The Inn at the Landing. One of the volunteers was a few months shy of legal drinking age. So the sisters forged a baptismal certificate so she could have a drink.

As several board members and volunteers piled into the restaurant, heads turned toward the group that included both a priest in flowing robes and hippies with flowing hair—all laughing and talking about what their official legal status might do for the kids.

For one thing, it expanded options for funding.

ORIGINAL BOARD OF DIRECTORS:

1. Father John Sharpe, C.M.
2. Mrs. Geneva Price
3. Mrs. Delores Haynes
4. Sr. Corita Bussanmas
5. Mr. Richard Koch
6. Mr. Brian Quinn
7. Mrs. Patricia Soden
8. Mrs. Anna Jennings
9. Mr. John Henry Haynes
10. Mrs. Willie Mae Burke
11. Mr. Peter Sandwall
12. Sr. Berta Sailer
13. Mr. Anthony Burke
14. Mr. R. L. Sweeny
15. Mrs. Mary Louise Bradley
16. Mrs. Phyllis Gillis
17. Mrs. Victoria Vappie
18. Mrs. Anita Bradford
19. Mr. Willie Banks
20. Mrs. Lena Rhodes

THE FIRST AUDIT

Claudia York now worked as the associate director of Model Cities Area 3 in the Leeds-Dunbar neighborhood. She had learned a great deal about the application process and recommended that Operation Break Through apply for funds now that it was bona fide nonprofit.

With help from Rich and Peter, Claudia went through the complicated application process that involved appealing to seven different boards. Parents of Operation Break Through students had to plead their cause at area meetings. Six out of seven voted to support Model Cities funding. During this time, the agency amended its name to Operation Breakthrough.

The school won conditional funding from Model Cities in 1971. It was a lifeline. Sr. Corita told the teachers they could start depositing their paychecks again. They could even hire more teachers, especially since most worked for $50 a week plus room and board in the nuns' convent.

To extend the Model Cities grant for the next year, the center had to submit to an audit to determine that "the fidelity bonding coverage, accounting, reporting and internal control systems meet the minimum requirements prescribed by the Accounting and Financial Management Procedures for the Execution Phase of the Model Cities Program." Representatives from Ernst & Ernst interviewed employees, observed them at work, and looked over the records.

During one visit, a chicken hopped up on the desk where the auditor was working and started clucking and pecking at papers.

"Could you get this damn thing off my desk?" he asked Connie Crumble, one of the teachers nearby. She feared the auditor would find something worse than chicken poop. Sr. Berta had been giving her paychecks with the warning, "Don't put this in the bank without asking me first." Two months had gone by, and Connie hadn't deposited her paychecks.

The Ernst & Ernst auditor was clearly not impressed with the chickens or the cuckoo-land accounting. On December 21, 1972, Samella Gates, director of the Model Cities Agency of Kansas City, Missouri, sent the results of the systems evaluation to Sr. Corita. The findings included:

1. *There is presently no fidelity bond coverage.*
2. *Purchase orders are not being used.*
3. *Voided checks have not been retained for subsequent inspection.*
4. *There are no written personnel policies.*
5. *In some instances, disbursements were not supported by invoices, receipts, or contracts.*
6. *The bank account was not reconciled properly.*
7. *The Operating Agency (O/A) does not have Federal, State of Missouri and City of Kansas City, Missouri, identification numbers for tax purposes. In addition, no documents were available for inspection to indicate that O/A is exempt from Federal income taxes and State of Missouri and Federal unemployment taxes. It was stated that the O/A had made application for all of the above items.*
8. *One of the check signers is not examining supporting documents prior to signing checks in all instances.*
9. *Daily receipts are not being deposited in the bank account on a timely basis.*
10. *Several clerical errors were noted during the review of the cash disbursements journal.*
11. *Supporting documents for cash disbursements were not filed in a manner that allowed them to be located easily. It is recommended that all supporting documents be affixed to an 8 ½" x 11" paper and be filed in numerical sequence by check number.*
12. *Internal control appears to be inadequate as the director signs checks, approves disbursements, prepares bank deposits, and performs all phases of the bookkeeping function.*

"Payroll transactions were not reviewed since the Operating Agency has not prepared or paid its own payroll in the past," the audit continued.

Prior to the audit, the Kansas City government, which had been sending local funds to the center, had concluded that getting ducks to chase mice would be easier than getting the nuns to keep a check register, so the city had taken over the task. Sr. Corita sent all bills to Howard Hoskins, who cut a check—and kept a record of it.

Sr. Berta reported that she heard Howard once say to someone, "If you give those damn nuns money, they'll spend it on the kids. They just don't care about the IRS."

The Ernst & Ernst audit went on to report:

Based upon our survey, the accounting, reporting, and internal control systems in their present state appear inadequate to comply with the standards set forth in Accounting and Financial Management Procedures for the Execution Phase of the Model Cities Program (CDA Letter No. 8, Part II, dated June 1969).

Sr. Corita shook her head and looked skyward, perhaps for the first time fully realizing all the work required to bring the organization into compliance.

Sr. Berta scowled at what she saw as time-wasting nonsense that would distract from helping families. Paperwork wasn't something she took at all seriously. She had more important things to master.

Fundraising wasn't the only skill the sisters had to acquire to keep the center going after they lost the diocese support. They had to provide their own bus service to pick up the children. They used some of their funds to purchase an old school bus.

SHIFTING GEARS

Willie Mae Burke already knew how to drive a bus, but regulations required that two adults who could both drive the bus accompany the children. Sr. Berta, whose driving skills regularly attracted the attention of the Kansas City Police Department, had never driven a car with a manual transmission, much less a bus, but she volunteered.

Helen Gragg's husband, John, who was a lifelong bus operator, said he could teach her.

Their first lesson was at Calvary Cemetery at 6901 Troost. John explained how the clutch worked and how and when to shift gears. Sr. Berta, who was more than a foot shorter than her six-foot, four-inch driving instructor, had trouble reaching the pedals. The bus seemed as big as an ocean liner as she prepared for her maiden voyage. The pastoral quiet was soon interrupted with grinding noises and clutch-clunking. The bus stuttered forward and, on more than one occasion, jumped a curb and rolled over someone's grave.

"May they rest in peace," said John, who was ever good-humored and patient.

"That's unlikely until I get out of here," quipped his pupil.

She learned to drive the bus on level ground but never quite mastered getting it up a hill. Sometimes, she rolled the bus all the way back down repeatedly before she got into a gear that would take it to the top.

Sr. Berta was always ready to learn a new skill or venture into a new endeavor—although she did not always attain mastery of them.

Sr. Berta made sure students celebrated every holiday

IT'S A GAS

The St. Vincent's church had operated a Standard Oil service station at 31st and Paseo for many years. In 1971, the older students started working at the station. Sr. Corita thought real-world job experience would be good for them. In early 1973, Sr. Berta learned that the church's lease on the station had ended.

"We could lease and run the gas station," she told Sr. Corita. "It would be an opportunity for the kids to learn more business skills. And it would provide money so we wouldn't be so dependent on Model Cities."

Standard Oil required a deposit of $4,000.

The sisters started calling on banks for a loan. Their habits, hoods, and crucifixes, which had worked so well on the IRS, did nothing for bank executives.

"No," "No," "No," they heard as they trudged from bank to bank. "You don't have any experience." "You don't have a business plan." "You don't have any visible means of repaying the loan." "The neighborhood is too dangerous." "The risk is too great."

"Who would rob two nuns running a gas station?" Sr. Berta asked him. They would soon find out.

After more than a dozen rejections, a wet-dog smell had begun to waft off their scratchy, black-serge habits. This put Sr. Berta in a despairing mood as they entered the office of Byron Thompson, senior vice president of First National Bank.

He listened to their story with a patient expression. "Sisters, there is no way the bank can make this loan," he said. "But my wife and I will."

With his check in hand, Operation Breakthrough signed an agreement to lease the station. The two sisters were going to learn how to pump gas.

Sr. Berta was confident the station would quickly begin to generate enough money to support the school.

Teachers took turns working gas-station shifts

Sr. Corita promoted Rich to station manager. Since he was one of a few male teachers, she thought he must know something about cars. This was mistake number one. Rich says:

I grew up in New York City. I didn't get a driver's license until I was a senior in college. My Volkswagen Beetle was my first car. Its motor is in the back, and the gas tank is in front. I couldn't even find the gas tanks in American cars.

I took a training course from Standard Oil. I went to tune-up and brake schools. I quickly realized there was no way I was going to work on cars.

Chuck Mercuri was an excellent mechanic, so he soon took over the job. His friend Carlos Chaves was at least mechanically inclined, so he started spending time at the station too. A customer asked him to rebuild a carburetor for his Olds Tornado, and he thought, *How hard can this be?* Chaves, who had dyslexia, asked his sister, Tamara, to read the manual to him. After a few oil spills, he mastered the technique.

All the staff, including Srs. Berta and Corita, took shifts pumping gas, checking oil, and washing windshields. So did the seventh- and eighth-grade students. They kept the books for the station, learning valuable accounting lessons along the way. They got some unplanned lessons in survival as well.

The station was open until around midnight in what had become a rough neighborhood. Sr. Berta's belief that nunly status would afford protection proved to be her second mistake in the gas business.

"Every single person there was tied up in the bathroom and robbed, except Corita and me," she said. "Everyone wanted to be on duty with Corita and me."

Carlos Chaves reported to the sisters that on a recent shift:

A guy pulled up who was really drunk. He said he needed oil. One of the kids on duty checked it and said, "It's fine."

"I know I'm a quart low," the guy screamed and started waving a gun at the kids. The two kids jumped into a Dumpster. I was shocked that they both knew exactly what to do.

Learning critical life skills wasn't just for students.

Peter Sandwall with students at the gas station

CHAPTER 9
FROM MODEL CITIES TO MODEL CITIZENS

School cook, Richard Chapman, and friend

Richard Chapman was running late for his job as a cook at Operation Breakthrough. He had stopped to watch the kids during a morning recess. Rain kept them indoors, so they put on a new Jackson 5 hit, "Rock Around the Clock," and danced in the hallways. Richard only made $53 a week, so he considered watching the kids enjoy themselves a perk of the job.

It wasn't the first time Richard was late; he was easily distracted. His red hair swirled around his face like a tangle of copper wire, earning him the nickname Red. His tall, lanky frame, torn blue jeans, and mustache gave him a too-cool-to-care look. He was thinking about how he could streamline the menu and serve hot dogs. This would suffice as lunch for the 200 children in the school and childcare programs.

When Richard encountered Sr. Corita, he started to apologize for being late, but she crossed her arms, tilted her head down, and locked her dark eyes on him in a way that cut him off mid-sentence.

After graduating high school in 1968, Richard became a conscientious objector to the Vietnam War. To fulfill the CO community requirement, he had worked in a hospital lab at the University of Kansas Medical Center. Richard says:

I hated it. I didn't do a very good job. I started missing work, and my boss fired me. I was a rebel, a hippie. I was hedonistic and self-destructive. Since I was violating the CO terms, the FBI arrested me for draft evasion. I spent a weekend in jail at the Federal Building. I had to find another job fast.

A friend told me about a position for a cook. My mother was an excellent cook. She volunteered her services at the church where we attended, and I used to help her. So I applied.

Yum, Yum One Dish, aka pasta casserole, was a student favorite

I fell in love with cooking at St. Vincent's. Most of our food products came from USDA surplus. I would have lots of cheese, butter, and soy extender. I'd make meatloaf with half beef and half soy, mac and cheese, and sloppy joes.

My meals had a Southern bent. If you did anything too weird, the children wouldn't eat it. One of their favorites was Yum, Yum One Dish Dinner (hamburger, frozen mixed vegetables, canned tomatoes, and rotini under melted cheese).

At the previous Thanksgiving, I roasted two turkeys. As I took them out of the oven, the hot pan slid down on my forearms. I wanted to drop it, but I couldn't because those turkeys were for the kids. Sometimes, though, because I was young and full of life, I would be less enthusiastic.

After a few seconds of staring, Sr. Corita shook her head and said, "Richard, if you fail, you don't fail me. You fail the kids."

Sr. Corita was a Buddha-like figure whom he never wanted to disappoint. Her message would stay in his mind, as long as the scars have on his forearms.

Sr. Corita regularly patrolled the hallways to keep an eye on both the teachers and the kids. On one occasion, a child handed her a plastic baggie. She started to ask the boy to throw it in the trash, but Richard, who was nearby, said, "Keep it. It's a lid of marijuana. I think I know who is selling it."

A judge had called the school and asked the nuns to take in a young man who had gotten into trouble in California. The judicial community knew of their willingness to take in out-of-control kids. Sr. Berta, especially, had a soft spot for troublemakers. "Who will love them if I don't?" she would say about particularly difficult cases. Few of the staff, including Sr. Corita, had Sr. Berta's tolerance for misbehavior.

Richard discovered that this young man was selling dope out of the art room to several delivery people and a few of the parents. He chased him out the front door until the kid jumped onto a city bus and disappeared.

Srs. Berta and Corita believed that doing good would raise the tide of humanity. They instilled a sense of purpose. They sure put me on a right path in life.

—Richard Chapman, former cook

The sisters didn't shut people down. They never expelled or even suspended anyone. They never, ever gave up on any of us.

—Kim Randolph, school alumna

Most infractions weren't as serious. Kim Randolph says:

In seventh grade, four of us girls collected makeup from our mothers, who all had cases of Fashion 220. I brought a tube of cobalt-blue eye shadow. We crowded into the girls' restroom and put on eyeliner, eye shadow, foundation, and lipstick. Sr. Corita saw us walk into a classroom and followed us in with a look that said, No way. She scared us with her expression.

She took us straight to the bathroom and washed off the makeup with brown paper towels. And while she was doing it, she made us see how silly we looked.

Sr. Corita could also show great compassion.

LEAP TO ACTION, NOT JUDGMENT

One of the eighth-grade girls started gaining weight. Her classmates teased her about being pregnant. Her parents came to the same conclusion and threatened to kick her out of the house. Then the BVM motherhouse got word and ordered Sr. Corita to figure out a way to cover it up. She says:

I thought we should not be worrying about hiding this situation but about how to get this child some medical attention so we could figure out what we were dealing with.

Sr. Berta took the girl to a doctor, who discovered the girl had a tumor. She took her to St. Joseph Hospital, where she underwent surgery. Then Berta brought her home and nursed her back to health.

The kindness of the sisters became a beacon for those in trouble, and enrollment at the school ballooned. So did the waiting list. Turning away students deeply pained the sisters, but the city had been decreasing its funding, so Sr. Corita appealed to the Kansas City Council in 1973:

When we were first funded, we had about 95 students. In the last two years, our enrollment has increased to 210 students, with 40 on our waiting list. As our enrollment has increased each year, the financial aid we have requested from the city has decreased.

…Our basic problem is to help children who are so often in need of an alternative school. We find we are dealing with many families who do not have the financial assets to completely support a school. Therefore, we are asking the city to continue to help us. We realize that city funds are scarce and that the city has many needs and problems and financial demands. We also realize that the city values its children. We are asking you, Mayor Wheeler, and the members of the City Council for your continued support in this project.

Kansas City granted funds from the Model Cities program for another year. Then, in 1974, the program ended nationally.

Stephanie Palmer

THE CLASS OF 1974

The eighth graders who graduated from Operation Breakthrough in 1974 reflected the promise of Model Cities. "Young, Gifted, Black," "Look Natural, Express Yourself, See It Like It Is" they advised on a photo page of smiling young adults. Their desired careers included teacher, policeman, fire chief, doctor, psychiatrist, dancer, electronic engineer, nurse, airline stewardess, and veterinarian.

The yearbook listed the graduates' favorite music, cars, TV programs, subjects, and future plans, among other things.

Stephanie Palmer spent her seventh and eighth grades at St. Vincent's. Her parents feared that their rambunctious and highly social daughter might wind up in a wild crowd that dominated the public middle school she was supposed to attend. They thought the rigorous structure of a parochial school would give her a few more years of childhood. She agreed to attend St. Vincent's school if two of her friends could come as well. Her entry in the 1974 yearbook was:

Singing group: Spinners
Car: Gran Torino Elite
TV program: "Goodtimes"
Plans for the future: I would love to finish school and go to college. I want to become either a lawyer or a computer programmer.

A page of prophecies listed hers as:

"Ms. Stephanie Palmer is the only woman owner and coach of a professional baseball team called the Kansas City Strykers. Stephanie has taught each of her players how to hold and use a bat. The team has an unusual record—no one has ever hit a ball." (The softball team she played on for two years lost every game.)

Dwayne Ivory Bradford's entry was:

Singing group: The Stylistics
Car: Monte Carlo
TV program: "Goodtimes"
Plans for the future: I plan to be a basketball player.

His prophecy was:

"Dwayne Bradford is the owner of a company called 'Small Things, Inc.' This company manufactures small things to throw for school boys who don't have time to make spitballs."

1974 school yearbook

The graduates of the last class funded through Model Cities held their ceremony at the Linwood Multipurpose Center. All the boys wore suits and the girls dresses. Among the graduation gifts from their parents were Princess phones, typewriters, and record players.

In 1975, the city awarded the school and daycare funds from general revenue sharing. The center also got funds for remedial reading and math through Title I. Additional funds from Title XX and the Comprehensive Employment and Training Act (CETA), signed into law by President Richard Nixon in 1973, helped keep the doors open.

The school submitted an application for funds from the Missouri Law Enforcement Association in 1975. By then, the school had 205 students—95 percent of whom were black and 48 percent of whom were girls, according to a report Sr. Corita prepared to apply for the funds. The operation also depended on money from the candy sales.

The tuition was $300 a year, but many parents were unable to afford it. The nursery charged $20 a week.

Sr. Corita's report said the school was taking increasingly problematic children as area organizations—such as Youth Service Center, Juvenile Court, Missouri Mental Health Center, and Rebound Program—had begun to refer students to Operation Breakthrough.

The report also cited that a majority had "a history of truancy, aggressive behavior toward their peers, hostility toward authority, and serious deficiencies in the basic subject areas." Parents whose children were not adjusting to traditional schools also turned to Operation Breakthrough for help.

Despite these challenges, the school documented a track record of successes. For the previous four years, 90 percent of graduates attended regular high schools. "Only 3 percent have had any further contact with law enforcement agencies," it stated. Test scores showed that the students' improvement rates were better than average. A group of 10 students, randomly selected, were given the Iowa Test of Basic Skills in April 1974 and again a year later. Results showed improvement rates of about a year and a half in all three subject areas: reading, math, and language.

The report included case studies, such as a 15-year-old the Youth Service Center sent to Operation Breakthrough in September 1974. It stated:

Carl had been enrolled in Westport High School in 9th Grade. Carl was all but illiterate and, as a result, was causing serious problems in school and had a history of school adjustment... Carl has had several occasions of violent behavior at school, including physically attacking others. His tantrums and erratic behavior have resulted in several suspensions.

...Carl came here very frustrated with school but amazingly he still had a great desire to learn to read. A survey of Carl's reading needs was taken and he began to learn basic reading skills. His whole attitude changed as he found himself able to read simple sentences. Carl thrived and developed positive relationships with his teachers.

...He learned to discuss his feelings instead of just giving in to a temper tantrum. Carl graduated in June and will probably attend De La Salle Education Center. Carl is leaving here with a positive attitude toward school and toward himself.

His Iowa Test of Basic Skills improved over the course of one year from 4.0 in reading; 3.3 in language; and 3.9 in math, to 6.8 in reading; 7.7 in language; and 5.4 in math.

The report also cited Shelby, who came to the school at the age of seven, after his father felt he wasn't progressing in public school. It said:

Shelby was not learning. He was constantly disruptive in the classroom and had begun to be a problem at home. The report sent to us from the public school indicated that "Shelby steals, does not tell the truth, has no interest in his work, and no respect for authority."

Students formed lifelong friendships

The sisters worked with Shelby's parents to focus more on praising his attempts to motivate himself rather than using corporal punishment on his negative behaviors. Together, they created an individual plan of study. Soon, he was working at grade level and was able to "direct his own behavior." He also participated in all team sports, which provided a "healthy outlet for many of his energies." On his Iowa Test of Basic Skills, he went from scores in 1974 of 1.2 in reading; 1.4 in language; and 1.8 in math, to scores in 1975 of 3.5 in reading; 3.9 in language; and 3.0 in math.

The third student profiled in the report was a 15-year-old who lived in the Wayne Minor Housing Projects with his mother and several brothers and sisters. Larry had attended Lincoln Junior High in special education classes. He had a history of poor school performance and frequent displays of "very aggressive behavior." The juvenile court system referred him to Operation Breakthrough. The report stated that Larry had "an almost complete absence of reading and math skills," with no desire to improve. The open program at the sisters' school gave him the freedom to approach learning in areas of his interests, which were science and art. It said:

As Larry began to relax and relate positively with other students, Larry also started to spend some time in the Math and Reading room working on contracts developed for him. Because the program is individualized, Larry could work at his own pace without the pressure of competition and "trying to keep up with the other kids."

Larry began to see his own progress and as he did he was motivated to work even harder to master skills that previously he felt were impossible. Larry also participated in the school's basketball and track teams. Larry has built confidence in himself as an individual who is capable of achieving goals he sets for himself. He has learned to accept himself and others and has a more positive approach to life.

Summer activities included an archaeology dig

Mayor Charles B. Wheeler, Jr., wrote a letter of support dated July 21, 1975. He described the school over the last four years as having "become very beneficial to the residents of the central city. The school's program is valuable to our community, and I am pleased to lend my support. I hope favorable consideration will be given to your application for funds."

The city must have been impressed because it increased the funding enough to keep the doors open for another year.

POST-GRADUATE PROBLEMS

With a few more dollars, the nuns tried to expand services to solve new problems. As children graduated, they didn't stop turning to the sisters with their woes.

After Kim Randolph graduated in 1973, she went to Bishop Lillis High School at 3737 Troost. It was more conservative and more structured, and Kim didn't adjust well. She missed the hands-on teaching and the personal interaction with teachers. She started failing classes.

"Lillis feels like a cold world," Kim told Sr. Berta. "I don't feel like anyone cares about me or knows me or even wants to know me. I hate it. You have to wear uniforms. There are so many rules. I miss St. Vincent's."

Sr. Berta knew of a program where the city would pay organizations to hire teenagers to do community service. Kim could help with the daycare kids, making breakfast and lunch and taking them to the playground. She could come back to the place she loved and make some spending money too. Before considering the finer points of the arrangement, Sr. Berta offered her a job.

"You were supposed to be at least 15 years old, but I was only 14," Kim said. "So Sr. Berta and my mother marched down to the Social Security office to try to change my birthdate."

When Sr. Berta saw a problem, she wanted to fix it. No one was going to be left out or turned away under her watch, no matter what she had to do. In Sr. Berta's world, people sometimes had to break some rules to make an omelet.

CHILDREN COUNT; SO DO INSPECTORS

Each year, the Missouri Department of Health and Welfare (MDHW) granted the daycare a license based on space and the ratio of staff to children. In 1973, the report to the licensing bureau listed two co-directors— Sr. Berta, who took no salary, and Anna Jennings, who made about $70 a week. It also included one teacher (Mary L. Bradley), five teachers' aides, a maintenance woman (Victoria Vappie), and a cook (Richard Chapman), who also served the school kids. Also on the list were two volunteers (Sister Anne Lillie and Sr. Corita). Based on having a dozen adults on hand, the childcare license limited enrollment to 41.

However, not all the children came every day. Rather than turn away kids, the sisters over-enrolled, figuring a few would be absent when the inspectors came to count children. This worked *sometimes*, but most of the kids loved coming, and there were often a few too many.

The sisters found it impossible to turn children away, even when they did not have the staff to meet MDHW requirements. Thus, they were sometimes "over ratio." The state inspected the center quarterly but not on a predictable schedule.

Anna Jennings was as happy to see the inspector at the door as Patty Hearst was to see the Symbionese Liberation Army, because there were at least 10 too many students that day. She smiled and started talking loudly enough to trigger something known around the center as the "emergency field trip."

Teacher Mary Bradley taking students on "emergency field trip" to evade inspectors

As soon as Sr. Berta heard Anna's "field trip voice," she called one of the childcare aides and asked for someone she knew wouldn't be there, or she might say in a hushed whisper, "Time for an outing." These communications signaled that an inspector had come to do a count.

"I knew that meant I had to move a couple of kids out of the classroom, fast, and keep them out for an hour," said Connie Crumble, who joined the center in 1974 to teach kindergarten. Sometimes, aides took children to the park or to get ice cream. Willie Mae Burke sometimes took them by bus to the zoo.

Today, it was raining, so Sr. Berta asked the cleaning lady to stand in a play area to make the legal adult-to-child ratio. Sr. Corita says:

We never knew when an inspector would come. So we were always on guard. We never overloaded the building. The kids were always safe. We were very conscious of fire, having seen the aftermath of Our Lady of the Angels in Chicago.

The children were always happy to comply because they knew that wonderful things were likely to happen when they left the center.

HIGH-WIRE ACTS AND HIGH NOTES

Sr. Berta grew up in a joyless home. Her mother had disappeared, leaving her with a grandmother who worked full-time and didn't have much energy to spare for entertaining her young, rambunctious charge. Sr. Berta, a creative and imaginative child, knew what it felt like to be starved for adventures. She was not going to allow this to happen to the children under her watch. Every month, she came up with an activity just for fun.

"The sisters took us places that other kids in the African-American community didn't go," Kim Randolph says. In 1971, she got to see *Madama Butterfly* at

Connie Crumble teaching a kindergarten class

We were a team. We did what we needed to do.

—Sylvia Bagby, who took care of toddlers

the Lyric Opera. She was lost in the story about the callow naval officer who takes young Cho-Cho-San as a temporary bride then leaves her behind, pregnant with his child. Kim's father was stationed abroad, and she thought of him every time Lieutenant Pinkerton was on stage.

Kim cried at the part where the lieutenant returns to Japan with his American wife, and Cho-Cho-San realizes she must raise her baby alone. When the curtain fell, Kim turned, wide-eyed, to Sr. Berta and said, "Can we see it again?"

During her time at St. Vincent's, she saw the planetarium, the Ice Capades, the Nelson-Atkins Museum of Art, and the Kansas City Symphony. Kim says:

We'd also go fishing, to petting zoos, and anything Sr. Berta thought we'd enjoy. At a golf tournament, Sr. Berta asked the organizers if we could ride in the carts. Sometimes, she'd pull over at a construction site and say, "Let's watch the diggers dig." We'd pass a lake, and she'd take us to feed the fish.

Every year, volunteers would make hundreds of sandwiches and take the whole school and the daycare kids to the circus. Plus, there were regular trips to the Lake of the Ozarks.

Most of the kids in our neighborhood had never been outside the city.

While the sisters concentrated on expanding the children's horizons, a local preacher was about to limit their own.

Student fashion show

Dwayne Ivory Bradford and Bernard Rhoades

CHAPTER 10
A PISTOL-PACKING PASTOR

The diocese wanted Annunciation (top) and Holy Name to merge with St. Vincent's

The Reverend Frank Wright, wearing his customary black suit, huffed down the walkway from the St. Vincent's church to pay a call on Sr. Corita in the school building next door. The slight, 50-ish man stopped to compose himself before walking into her office.

Sr. Corita had been expecting him. She was surprised to find that he looked more like an undertaker than a preacher, but she was anxious to hear what he had to say.

For about five years, Operation Breakthrough had been paying a nominal monthly rent to the Diocese of Kansas City-Saint Joseph for use of the St. Vincent rectory and school properties after the consolidation in 1971.

In May 1975, the diocese notified the St. Vincent parish that it planned to merge parishes as well. According *The Catholic Key*, the consolidated site would be located at Annunciation (Linwood and Benton). The diocese would sell all its real estate at Holy Name and St. Vincent's, including the school and rectory, which housed the daycare.

When Srs. Berta and Corita learned of this development, they visited Bishop Helmsing at the chancery.

"Operation Breakthrough has an interest in buying the school property," Sr. Corita told him. He just laughed at them. Perhaps he knew of the organization's dire financial straits.

In June 1975, the Vincentian order locked the doors at the St. Vincent's church for good and signed over the deed to all its real estate at 31st and Flora to the diocese. This was more a burden than a bounty for the diocese because it came with a debt of $79,766 and an aging stone behemoth in need of a few million dollars in repairs.

The diocese must have been eager to unload it. Only a few weeks later, a letter arrived notifying Operation Breakthrough that the diocese had signed a one-year lease, with an option to buy, to Rev. Wright for all of its St. Vincent properties. The deal included the church, school building, rectory, and gas station, according to an article in *The Kansas City Times* dated August 2, 1975.

WRIGHT IS WRONG

Rev. Wright's newly formed Church of God in Christ had been meeting in a storefront at 24th and Olive for the past 18 months. The move into the grandly Gothic limestone structure, the second-largest Catholic church in the city, was quite a step up for the plucky Rev. Wright.

The sounds of tambourines, a saxophone, and a piano, along with a whole lot of *hallelujahs*, soon replaced the sedate Mass services. At the first service Wright conducted on August 1, 1975, he told the congregation of his dreams for the property. He saw it as a haven for the community, with senior housing in the old rectory.

The parishioners, who didn't begin to fill the 800 seats, shouted, "Amen!"

Sweeping his arm across the expansive nave and up to the 69-foot-high cedar ceiling, he boomed, "Thank you, Jesus! From somewhere, God sent this place. You see what God has done for you!"

Rev. Wright would soon lament what two Catholic sisters would do to his ambitions. Sr. Corita says:

Rev. Wright announced he was there to see about transferring the city grants from Operation Breakthrough to the Church of God in Christ. I told him, "The city is funding our program, not the church. We applied for those funds, and we control them. They are earmarked for Operation Breakthrough."

"We'll see about that," Rev. Wright said as he stomped out of my office. "I'm going to City Hall right now to ask that the city transfer the Operation Breakthrough contract to me."

One can only imagine the conversation that took place between the Rev. Wright and the city administrator who informed him that the funding belonged to the organization, not the building. Finding out that Sr. Corita was correct did not improve the reverend's relations with the sisters.

Landlord lockout created chaos at school and daycare

The next time Rev. Wright came calling, he raised the rent. He wanted $500 a month for the school and $300 a month for the convent and rectory. Sometimes, city funds were delayed, and the sisters couldn't pay the rent on time, which further irked the reverend.

The next time he visited, he was shouting, "I want you out of here, *now!* Do you hear me?" Sr. Corita reports that he took a pistol out of his robes and banged it three times on her desk as he said, "Out, out, *out!*"

Rev. Wright wasn't the only man of the cloth in the neighborhood to pack a pistol, but he was more likely than most to use it to make a point.

Sr. Corita smiled benevolently at him. Rev. Wright filed a suit against the sisters for non-payment of rent and began eviction proceedings in the fall of 1976. According to an article in *The Kansas City Times* dated October 12, 1976, there was an "imminent crisis" at Operation Breakthrough.

"I don't know whether, come November 1, we will be moving out of here or what will happen," Sr. Corita said.

That night, several volunteers and board members gathered at the Pink House to discuss the new development.

They all agreed to start looking for alternative locations and to come up with a strategy to stay at 31st and Flora until they found one.

FROZEN OUT

For a while, Rev. Wright didn't pay much attention to the sisters. The duties of running a congregation must have distracted him. The first signs of trouble happened in early November when Sr. Berta arrived at the school building one chilly morning to discover there was no heat. The utility company had shut off the gas for failure to pay. Sr. Berta says:

We paid him money for gas, and he never paid the gas bill. The childcare center in the convent and the rectory were on another account and had their own heating systems, which were still working. But the heater for the school was in the church basement. Rev. Wright was trying to freeze us out. I was worried about the kids in the cold classrooms, so I went out and bought three propane tanks and managed to hook them up to run the boiler in the church basement. The smell was awful, but it kept the kids from freezing to death.

The tanks were expensive, so Sr. Berta started knocking on parents' doors, asking if they could contribute to the propane fund. The situation with Rev. Wright was deteriorating. He had started patrolling the street, eyeing the rectory to determine whether anyone was inside.

LOCKED OUT

The sisters had only time for a quick glance at the newspaper before starting their day on Tuesday, November 23, 1976. The top stories were about President Gerald Ford meeting with his successor, Jimmy Carter, to plan an orderly transition, how the proposed Kansas budget might outrun revenues, and how ducks had led zookeepers on a wild goose chase.

Sr. Berta's eye caught a story about a program at an inner-city school in Chicago that was helping students improve their reading skills. It involved getting parents to sign contracts to read to their children.

"We need to develop a handbook about this for our parents," she said to Sr. Corita. They were deep into this discussion when they arrived at the school to find all the doors padlocked, two days before Thanksgiving.

"This is nuts," Sr. Berta said. "What are we going to tell the 200 children who will be arriving any minute?"

"Out of evil has to come good," Sr. Corita said cryptically. "We'll just convince Rev. Wright to open these doors."

"Just how are we going to do *that*?"

"Berta, you've got to find the good," Sr. Corita said. "You can if you try. Anything people do is because they want to be good, even if it might not seem like it to us. Remember…"

Sr. Berta finished her sentence. "Nothing is so bad that it can't be worse." Then she headed off to bang on the back door of the rectory, where the Rev. Wright lived. There was no answer.

"We'd better check the front door of the rectory," said Sr. Berta. Sure enough, there was a padlock on the door where mothers would soon be bringing 28 infants and toddlers who were enrolled in the Operation Breakthrough childcare program.

"What in the world are we going to do?" they said in duet.

Stephanie Palmer and Rebecca Reed

The sisters soon discovered that Rev. Wright had left the convent open. Sr. Berta left a note on the rectory telling the moms to report to the convent at 3121 Paseo, where aides took care of 50 preschool students.

With the help of the moms and the aides, they made room for the babies on the second floor of the convent. As they settled them in drawers and boxes, Sr. Corita prayed that inspectors from the Missouri Division of Family Services wouldn't show up that day.

"This is against the law," Sr. Berta told the adults who were helping to bundle up the babies in their makeshift bassinets. "But what choice do we have?"

Meanwhile, the teachers were corralling the students, who ranged in age from five to 15, in front of the school. They all chattered with excitement. Some hoped for an early Thanksgiving vacation, but Sr. Corita was not about to send more than 200 kids back to empty homes when so many parents were already at work.

Sr. Corita started calling nearby churches and centers, hoping to find temporary shelter, but it was still before 8:00 a.m., and no one answered. Finally, she reached someone at the Linwood Multipurpose Center. Yes, the children could come with their teachers to the building at 3200 Wayne, only two blocks away.

The teachers had no books, supplies, desks, or chairs, but they had imagination, and the children had a roof over their heads. They sang songs, asked students to read aloud from their own schoolbooks, and staged informal debates. The din in the large meeting hall rivaled that of a Rolling Stones concert, but the teachers managed to keep the kids entertained for two days until the Thanksgiving holiday.

After their first day as refugees, the sisters realized that Rev. Wright could lock them out of the convent or even their home at any minute.

That night, Sr. Berta told the group of teachers, parents, and hippie volunteers huddled around their coffee table, "We need to stage a sit-in. Rev. Wright can't lock us out as long as there are people inside. We need to make sure we never leave the convent or our house empty."

Anna Jennings agreed to stay in the convent, and the hippies agreed to make sure there was always someone at the Pink House, so Rev. Wright couldn't padlock the doors.

"Does anyone know how to pick locks?" Sr. Berta asked. "We've got to figure out how to get all of our stuff out of those buildings."

The Linwood Multipurpose Center provided emergency shelter after the lockout

"First we need somewhere to go," Sr. Corita said.

Rich Koch promised to find out what was available to rent in the area. Rich had stopped teaching classes at the school to go to law school at the University of Missouri-Kansas City. But he still served on the center's board and was ready to spend his Thanksgiving holiday helping the sisters.

"We have to find someplace before Monday," Sr. Berta reminded him.

That night, the sisters moved their mattresses off the beds and onto the floor because they were afraid Rev. Wright might shoot through their windows.

Last Easter celebration for children at St. Vincent's in 1975, just before the diocese leased the parish to the Church of God in Christ

CHAPTER 11
NIGHT MOVES

Former FAA building became a second
home to Operation Breakthrough
(Photo from FAA)

Rich Koch started combing the real estate ads. He stopped at every "For Rent" sign and made inquiries. Then he saw an item about a building at 4825 Troost that had formerly housed the Federal Aviation Administration (FAA) offices. The University of Missouri-Kansas City wanted to buy it but didn't have the funds to consummate the deal. Rich had a hunch about how to approach the buildings' owners.

On Thanksgiving day, Rich, Sr. Berta, and Sr. Corita toured the property with Ted H. Greene, who co-owned the building with J. Russell Gramlich.

The property was 132,087 square feet—more than two football fields. The building was 78,758 square feet, about the same size as the Smithsonian's Arts and Industries Museum. Inside was the first computer the sisters had ever encountered. It took up the space of four offices. Srs. Berta and Corita looked at each other as if they had just seen the devil.

After the intimate spaces of St. Vincent's, the inside of 4825 Troost looked like a vast prairie. Sr. Corita wanted to know what the utility costs were—$10,000 per month in the summertime. Sr. Berta imagined all the activities and services they could provide.

Greene and Gramlich had acquired the property on May 1, 1973, from the FAA. For almost three years, it had sat empty.

"The property taxes on this must be pretty high," Rich said to Ted. "If you rented it to a nonprofit organization, you might get an exemption from real estate while you are trying to sell the building to UMKC."

They struck a deal. Operation Breakthrough signed a lease for the property beginning December 1, 1976, only five days away. The rent was a dollar a month, and Operation Breakthrough had an option to purchase the building.

"Thank goodness, we won't be nomads as long as Moses was," Sr. Berta said.

Operation Breakthrough now had a vast space…and nothing to put in it. Rev. Wright had locked up all of their desks, books, tables, lab equipment, beakers, sports equipment, cafeteria utensils, cots, mats, toys, and bedding.

Staff quickly set up a makeshift playground at the new location

WHAT'S MINE IS MINE

The sisters spent their evenings at their new building, trying to get it ready to pass inspection as a daycare. The school students were already there, in classrooms the sisters created by marking them off with duct tape on the floor. They also taped off a track around the perimeter of the huge room so the track teams could practice indoors.

The teachers had a hard time maintaining order because the students paid no attention to the duct-tape boundaries. Kids roller-skated and played tag, careening around the space like bumper cars. The teachers longed for the supplies and games that would keep the kids quiet—the ones locked up at St. Vincent's.

"If we had certified teachers, they would all lose their minds," Sr. Corita wryly observed to Sr. Berta one night after spending a few days in the new location. Both the teachers and students missed all the books, toys, and learning materials from the building on Flora.

Sr. Corita had made several attempts to contact Rev. Wright to retrieve their equipment from the locked buildings. She says:

He seemed not to care about anything other than evicting us. We were still running the daycare in the convent. We heard that he had tried to convince the police to put out an arrest warrant on us for trespassing. He showed up at the convent just before parents were supposed to pick up their kids and told me if I didn't stop trespassing on his land, he would shoot me. This time he had a shotgun and a chain. I started walking down the driveway. When I looked back, he was chaining the door—with the kids inside, just as the first moms came for their babies.

As I headed home to call the police, he walked behind me with the gun pointed at me, yelling that I had no right to be on his property.

Srs. Berta and Corita moved to escape the reverend

The scene unfolded in slow motion as she proceeded deliberately, with her statuesque posture and regal bearing about 20 feet ahead of the gun-waving pastor. Behind him was a group of panicked-looking moms demanding that he unlock the building so they could get their kids.

Rev. Wright couldn't convince the policeman who showed up to arrest Sr. Corita. When the officer told him he could go to jail for chaining up a building with people in it, Rev. Wright finally took the padlock off the convent door.

The sisters turned again to David Kierst for legal help. They also rented a house at 3617 Southwest Trafficway, a two-story clapboard home with a fenced backyard. It was far enough from Rev. Wright to make them feel safer at night.

David was able to get a court order to force Rev. Wright to allow the sisters to retrieve their belongings. Sr. Berta says:

We had to give him a list of everything that belonged to us. We set a day in early 1977, about a month after he locked us out of the school and rectory. At the appointed time, several of the parents and older boys showed up to help with the move. It was cold that day. The group of about 15 included Willie Mae Burke, Shirley Knighton, Ida Pelton, Anna Jennings, Helen Gragg, Anita Bradford, Mattie Flanagan, and Mae Richardson—not exactly professional movers.

Rev. Wright patrolled the scene like a prison warden. He kept bellowing, "You can't have the electric typewriters. You can't have the safe. You can't move it."

All of the materials and equipment belonged to us. We didn't steal anything. In fact, he had stolen some of our stuff.

Ms. Flanagan's son Cornelius was sitting in an office chair, and Rev. Wright said, "I own the office furniture. That doesn't go."

Cornelius said, "Yes, I know that." As soon as the reverend walked away, Cornelius rolled another 15 feet down the hall. The reverend would return and say, "Remember, that doesn't go."

Cornelius would reply, "I'm just sitting in it."

Rev. Wright's interference slowed down the process considerably, and the group feared it would take all night. After the sun set, Srs. Berta and Corita concocted a scheme to neutralize him. Sr. Corita excused herself. First, she headed for the office, where she kept a flashlight. Then she went to the basement and took all the fuses, leaving the building in darkness.

As Sr. Corita made her way back, she heard the reverend say, "What happened to the lights?"

"Must be an electrical short," Sr. Berta said. "It happens all the time." Fortunately, the darkness masked her sly smile.

The reverend, unfamiliar with the school's layout, said he would try to get to the basement to see if he could figure out what happened. After he left, the nuns whispered to their crew to continue the move.

"We told them, *This stuff is ours. We're not stealing anything,*" Sr. Berta says. "Rev. Wright was wrong; he locked us out."

"We thought the kids would get scared in the dark building, but they seemed to have night vision," Sr. Corita says. They knew the building pretty well and helped bring most of the contents of the school into a classroom on the northwest side of the building. They carried desks, chairs, books, cots, utensils, glassware, and trays from the cafeteria. The gas station just outside threw enough light into the classroom for the movers to pass things out a window. The ragtag crew loaded the stuff onto the school bus, which was moonlighting after hours as a moving van.

"Don't forget the safe," Sr. Berta hissed. "We may not have any use for it, but we want everything that belongs to us." The valiant group managed to get the safe, which weighed as much as a piano, up a flight of stairs and out the door.

Moving out the daycare furniture would happen in a much less dramatic fashion. Every day, the school-age children took buses to 4825 Troost from the daycare. They met in front of the convent at 3121 Paseo, where the daycare was still in operation. Sr. Berta says:

The driveway for the convent wasn't visible from the back door of the rectory, so we moved the daycare in secret. Every day, before the kids boarded the bus, an aide gave each one a piece of furniture or equipment. Then we'd tell them, "Sit on the bus and hold this chair in your lap until you get to school." The smaller children got blankets and lighter stuff, but the big kids sometimes had to ride with school desks on their laps.

Rev. Wright never noticed that a moving operation was happening under his nose.

Bus served double duty as moving van

Boa, the sneaky snake, was an adept escape artist

BYE-BYE, BOA

Sr. Berta had all kinds of ideas for how to make the former FAA offices look more inviting.

With help from some of the more construction-savvy volunteers, they put up framing for rooms, nailed wallboard, applied seam tape, and learned to trowel on joint compound.

"It was like icing cakes," Sr. Berta said. "And I wasn't so good at doing that either."

The teachers did their best to maintain order for the school-age children who were trying to study in the midst of scaffolding, blue plastic tarps covering mounds of materials, and jackhammering. Sr. Berta put up a Christmas tree whose lights flashed through a haze of construction dust.

To give the children some continuity, she brought some of the smaller animals, like hamsters and gerbils, from St. Vincent. The chickens went to an area farmer, but she couldn't do the same with the school's mascot, Boa. She installed the almost eight-foot-long snake in its cage on the second floor of 4825 Troost.

A Kansas City Health Department inspector didn't seem to mind the knee-deep plaster dust, jackhammers, or construction tools, but he feared the snake might escape and kill someone. And that is exactly what Boa almost did soon after, although not in the way the inspector imagined.

The next morning, while the sisters were debating what to do with Boa, the children noticed that the snake was hardly moving. One of the students had fed the snake a rat caught in the building a few days before. Sr. Berta feared the rat had eaten d-CON pellets that might harm Boa.

One of the volunteers and Willie Mae Burke, the designated driver for snakes as well as students, loaded Boa into the sisters' station wagon and took him to the zoo's veterinarian. On the ride home, Boa got out of his cage. He slithered through a hole in the vehicle's headliner fabric just above the cage. There was another hole in the fabric near the rearview mirror. When Boa poked his head through it, Willie Mae Burke drove off the road into a row of hedges. The two women, with the help of a windshield brush and newspapers, managed to coax the snake back into his cage.

The next trip to the zoo for Boa would be one way; he became an exhibit there.

The sisters often learned lessons the hard way. They found some Walt Disney wallpaper with Looney Tunes characters on it, like Bugs Bunny,

Daffy Duck, and Porky Pig. They thought the infants and toddlers would enjoy it.

And they weren't wrong. The kids began ripping the paper off the wall before the paste had even dried.

"Our toddlers must have the most advanced fine-motor skills in the country," Sr. Berta said. She and Sr. Corita spent the next few evenings steaming the rest of the paper off the walls and, afterward, opted for paint instead.

The sisters had to surmount several obstacles to get a daycare license for the new building. One was that the building did not have a kitchen, nor did the organization have a cook, but the center had to provide a hot lunch. After Rich Chapman and several other cooks quit, the sisters were doing the job. Sr. Berta reports one conversation she had with an inspector:

"How are you going to feed the children?" the inspector asked.

"Oh, we are going to cook in our home and bring the food to 48th Street."

"Do you have a catering license?" she asked.

"Yes." (Translation: We'll get one as soon as we can.)

"Do you have a refrigerated vehicle?"

"Yes." (I had a cooler with ice cubes.)

After several weeks of ferrying vats of sloppy joes and spaghetti from their home at 3117 Paseo to 4825 Troost, the sisters found a licensed and affordable caterer willing to feed 226 children.

The inspector had mandated a fenced-in playground. In a letter to the licensing bureau dated January 12, 1977, Sr. Corita assured officials that they would fence in the 69,000-square-foot playground.

The city provided some funding for playground equipment, but the sisters imagined something grander. They started researching playgrounds at the public library. In late June 1977, they purchased lumber, and the staff spent three weeks installing swings, slides, rope bridges, a fort, a tire maze, concrete drainage pipes for crawling through, and a Canadian roller, which they fashioned from two large spools used for electric cable. Sr. Berta says:

We built a jungle gym that had a flight of steps up to a platform that was probably 20 feet above the ground. We strung a trolley line and put a pulley on it that the kids could grab and slide down. It was an early zip line. The kids loved it. I think only one of them broke an arm.

They also spread 250 tons of sand, which the children soon started tracking into the building.

"It was a disaster," says Sr. Corita. However, having the fenced playground qualified the center for Title XX federal funding. Additional funding from the city enabled the center to build a chain-link fence around the parking lot and install a fire alarm system inside the building.

When the licensing bureau said the center couldn't use the second floor because there were no classrooms, the two sisters, along with four staff members, built them, and Rich wired them for electricity. Enrollment rose from 226 children to 331 in 1977.

The reputation of Operation Breakthrough began to grow to match its size. In the past, most support had come from neighbors, parents, and area businesses. For the first time, citywide groups began to take an interest.

Volunteers from the Junior League of Kansas City, Missouri, started appearing regularly. They brought books and read to the children. They sponsored Family Read Nights, where parents and children received a hot meal, listened to stories, and participated in literacy activities. The organization also sponsored Eating Fresh, where volunteers showed parents how to prepare healthy food. The higher profile of the center also attracted job seekers.

The work paid off for the owners as well. The city granted an exemption from real estate taxes on June 24, 1977.

A CALMING PRESENCE

Her seafoam-green caftan shimmered as Marilyn Driver walked through the door to apply for a job at Operation Breakthrough. At five feet, ten inches tall, the queenly-looking woman, complete with oversized, gold-hoop earrings and gold pendant chains, seemed more like Nefertiti than a daycare worker.

"What's your experience working with children?" Sr. Corita asked.

Marilyn told her about how, as the mother of two children, she had gotten involved in Parents as Teachers in St. Louis, where she had been living before her husband was transferred to Kansas City. She soon had a leadership position in the group.

"Are you prepared to be the best you can be, to treat these children with love, to teach them something?" Sr. Corita asked.

"Yes, ma'am," Marilyn said.

"Are you prepared never to lay a finger on these children in anger or leave them unattended?"

"Yes, ma'am."

"Are you prepared to treat these children as if they were your own?"

"Yes, ma'am."

"Are your prepared to change diapers?"

"Yes, ma'am."

Marilyn started on February 13, 1979. With her buttery laugh and wide smile, she calmed her first charges, babies from six weeks to 18 months. Then she stayed with them when they moved to the toddler group. She mesmerized them with her songs, stories, and learning schemes.

When she taught a unit on the importance of taking good care of animals, she didn't just talk. She took them to a pet store to pick out their own. They came back with a guinea pig dubbed Don-Don.

"Every morning, everyone gets to pet Don-Don,"

Marilyn Driver discovered her calling caring for toddlers

she told the class. While they stroked the furry creature, she talked about love, gentleness, and responsibility.

Her hugs were so therapeutic that children who went on to higher grades often stopped by Marilyn's classroom for a hug before going off to their own classes. So did the parents. For a brief moment, they felt cherished as Marilyn wrapped them in her caftan and whispered in their ear, "Have a blessed day."

Her hours were from 6:00 a.m. to 6:00 p.m., but she didn't mind. Besides, Sr. Corita was sending her to Penn Valley Community College to become a certified childcare worker. She also took regular classes at UMKC and Avila College. Marilyn says:

At this age, the kids could talk, learn, and follow me around. At first, it wasn't so much teaching as taking care of the children and making sure they were okay. The kids loved "The Little Engine that Could." That was an important message for them. We can do it if we try, just like the little engine.

As the staff started going to workshops, we learned that we could teach the two-year-olds the alphabet, manners, numbers. The more we went to workshops, the more we learned about how to present lessons.

I learned to listen carefully to the kids when they talked, and how to modify a child's behavior in a positive way. By observing and listening, I learned to see problems before they happened.

I'd tell the 20 kids in my class, "Treat people like you would like to be treated. I don't like it when you hit me. So I won't hit you, and please don't hit me."

The sisters were always checking to make sure we were applying the lessons—Sr. Berta especially. She liked to come into class and cradle the babies. The whole time, she is observing. She could just walk by the classroom and notice all kinds of things—if I was raising my voice, if I was down on the floor with the kids, as I should be, or standing back.

Marilyn was amazed at how Sr. Berta seemed to be everywhere at once and in command of every situation. Shortly after passing by Marilyn's classroom one

Sr. Berta is all-seeing when it comes to kids. If I stood up for a second to catch my breath from standing on my head to make the kids laugh, she would find me and ask, 'Are you doing enough to entertain these kids?'

—Patricia Thompson, former teacher and current facility manager

day, an aide brought a child up to Sr. Berta. She heard the wheezing asthma.

"Call 9-1-1," Sr. Berta said as she carried the child to the front door. As the paramedics lifted the child into the ambulance, she started to step up with him. "Are you his parent?" the paramedic asked her. "Unless you are, you can't ride in this ambulance."

She turned to Mae Richardson, the receptionist who had come outside to help, and said, "Ha! This guy thinks I'm going to send this child to the hospital without a familiar face." She jumped into the ambulance, and the paramedic didn't say another word.

"You don't mess with Sr. Berta," Mae told the paramedic as he closed the door.

Mae Richardson was studying to become a legal secretary at Penn Valley Community College. The school's work-study program had sent her to Operation Breakthrough in 1975. In 1977, she became the full-time secretary there. Although she didn't move around half as much as Sr. Berta, she always seemed to know what was going on around the center.

One of the mothers complained that her son cried a lot at night.

"Oh, I know why he's crying," she said. "He wants a jelly sandwich."

Sure enough, the next day, the mother told her it had worked like magic.

Other problems weren't as easy to fix.

Mae Richardson

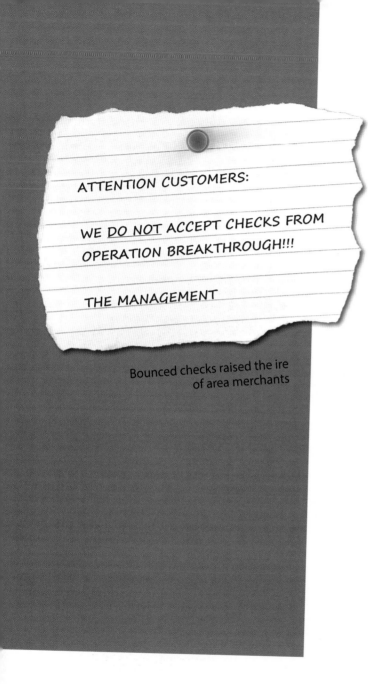

ATTENTION CUSTOMERS:

WE DO NOT ACCEPT CHECKS FROM OPERATION BREAKTHROUGH!!!

THE MANAGEMENT

Bounced checks raised the ire of area merchants

DUMPSTER DRIVING

With their real estate problems solved at least temporarily, the sisters began taking advantage of their expanded circumstances.

At St. Vincent's church, the daycare had a license for only about 40 children. By 1978, the center had a certificate of license for 24 infants and toddlers under age two and 82 preschoolers age two to six. The year before, the license had been issued for 24 infants and only 45 children.

The rapid growth of the center, as well as the sisters' habit of quickly putting every new dime toward bringing something new for the children, strained resources quickly.

Just paying the utility bills in the 78,758-square-foot building amounted to more than $15,000 a month, which ate up the bulk of the funding. In the late 1970s, the economy went into a recession, which meant fewer donations and less money to pay the staff.

"We didn't know from day to day whether we would be able to keep going," Marilyn says. Sr. Berta would hand her a paycheck and say, "Don't go to the bank; go to a grocery store."

Pretty soon, the grocery stores in the area put up stern notices: "We do not accept checks from Operation Breakthrough."

The sisters were usually the last to cash their checks. Employees would come into Sr. Corita's office and see her purse open on the floor, stuffed with unopened paychecks.

"I worked two months without getting paid," Connie Crumble said. "I knew the sisters would make good eventually. I was working for $60 a week. By the time I paid rent, I didn't have money to take the bus. The sisters let us bring our kids for free."

One day, five teachers—Marilyn, Connie Crumble, Cecelia Sevart, Lesa Flanagan, and Lola Flanagan—

We were all there to level the playing field for these children and their families.

—Kim Davis, former employee

waved their paychecks in the lunchroom, chanting a chorus of "No bank today, no bank today," and Sr. Berta came in scowling.

"She was on the lookout for attitude," Marilyn says. "We just shrugged and kept on going."

The women had something else to discuss—the kindergarten graduation the previous night. One by one the kids, clad in pint-size gowns, walked down the aisle with the gravity of brides. Connie announced their favorite foods and what they wanted to be when they were older.

"You wouldn't find that at another school," Cecelia said. Then they started teasing Connie about one of her favorite students, Barry Kountz. His mother reported that Barry had underlined her name in every phone book in the house.

"Oh dear, I'm going to miss him," Connie said. "He was a sweetheart and so inquisitive. I bet he asked me 1,000 questions."

"When they all sang that 'Magic Penny' song last night that you taught them, I melted," Cecelia said.

Love is like a lucky penny
Hold it tight and you won't have any
But, give it away
And you'll have plenty
You'll end up having more

"What's a paycheck compared to hearing something like that?" Cecelia said.

"We trusted in the sisters and what they were doing," Marilyn says. "We knew if we waited, we would get our money."

In a licensing application for 1979, St. Vincent's Childcare Center submitted its budget, written out in longhand. It estimated it would need $44,400, which was $2,177.22 under what it expected to receive. The center estimated it would take in $13,200 from Title VI funds from Kansas City and an optimistic $31,200

On February 1, 1978, an inventory reports possessions including:

3	vehicles (a 1976 Chevrolet Impala, a 1974 Ford Country Squire station wagon, and a 1974 International bus)
92	aluminum-plastic cots
90	blankets and sheets
1	baby bed
8	red plastic blocks
3	10-gallon glass aquariums
12	Formica tables
100	youth chairs
21	adult chairs
35	pinewood slats for shelving
108	cinder blocks for shelving
1	Norge VHQ washing machine
1	Sears Kenmore clothes dryer
1	Frigidaire freezer
1	Wells bread toaster

a year in fees from parents. The center charged parents $25 a week, but many couldn't afford this.

The sisters kept salaries perilously low. In 1978, the daycare center listed 19 employees and nine volunteers. Sr. Corita and Anna Jennings were co-directors. There were four teachers and several assistant teachers and teachers' aides. Sr. Berta was listed as the lead teacher. The total annual budget for all salaries was $38,688, an average of $2,036 per year per employee.

It was difficult, though, to attract candidates with good bookkeeping and business skills with compensation like this. Bills sometimes piled up like old newspapers in the office. The sisters knew how to calm a frightened child, unlock a child's desire to learn, and motivate a staff. But when it came to record-keeping, balancing budgets, and maintaining proper accounting practices, they were sorely lacking in both aptitude and interest.

"We took the bills and threw them in a box because we couldn't pay them anyway," Sr. Berta says. The Jackson County office of the Missouri Division of Family Services grew alarmed at the evidence of this cavalier approach to accounting.

When inspectors discovered that the same person opening the bills was also signing checks, with no oversight, they demanded the center hire a bookkeeper.

The sisters asked the county office to recommend someone. After several weeks of watching their new bookkeeper weave and wobble his way to his desk, then drop his head on it for hours at a time, the sisters both took a course in bookkeeping. At night, they struggled to learn a new language of ledgers.

"What's amortizing?" Sr. Berta asked Sr. Corita one night. "It sounds like something dangerous."

Corita laughed, and, after reading a section on "fiscal prudence," she said, "Berta, at least as nuns we know something about prudence. Or I do, anyway."

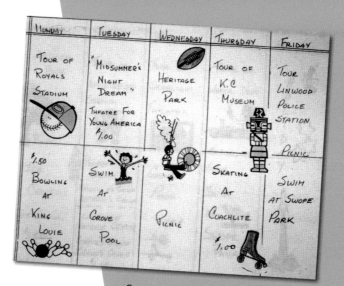

Summer schedule circa 1978

Swope Park swim

The sisters taught me how to be who God made me to be. They taught me how to be a better mother.

—Marilyn Driver, former teacher

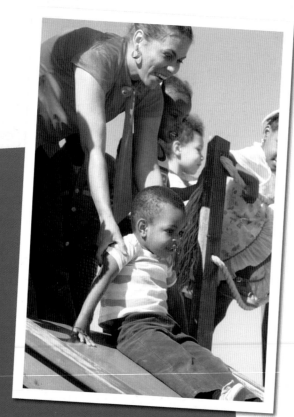

A city grant paid for a real playground

Accounting would not be their only distraction as the center grew.

"Sister, they've taken the Dumpster," Mae Richardson reported to Sr. Corita one day. The center had failed to pay the trash removal provider, so it removed the Dumpster. After hours, Srs. Berta and Corita put the trash in the back of their station wagon and drove around Kansas City, adding a bag here and there to other people's trash. They soon became knowledgeable about neighborhood trash schedules.

The staff did their best to keep expenses down. The teachers all cleaned and mopped their own rooms. In the process, though, they grew into compassionate caregivers. Marilyn says:

I painted boards and stacked bricks to make bookshelves and made a bulletin board with different feelings. I'd tell the kids, "Show me how you feel." I'd cut out faces with different expressions and post them on a bulletin board. I tried to develop ways for them to deal with everyday life.

The kids were always asking me, "Where do you live? What does your house look like? Can we come live with you?" So I planned a field trip to my house. I wrote up a lesson plan to study families and houses. How do different families live, what would you have in a home? What is the same, and what is different between homes? They learned shapes from windows and directions from stairs going up and down.

Every Wednesday, she took her students to the United Methodist church in Mission, Kansas, where parishioners read to the kids, helped with art projects, sang songs, and provided a snack.

Marilyn seemed to usher in a brief period of calm. For two more years, the center operated without calamity. The Division of Family Services increased the center's capacity in 1981 to 139 children ages six weeks to six years, with no more than 24 under age two. There were also still about 150 school-age students.

AN OFFER OR A THREAT?

In the early spring of 1981, Ted Greene called Sr. Corita. UMKC had finally made an offer on the building the nuns had been leasing for a dollar a year. Sr. Corita says:

He told me, "If you can come up with the money, I am giving you the option to buy it first."

"What's the price?" I asked.

"$6 million."

"There is no way we could pay for it," I told him. The entire budget of the organization was still under $50,000.

"Don't make us evict you," he said.

CHAPTER 12

JUGGLING PLATES AND PLACES

Babies didn't go hungry even after caterers vanished

Sr. Berta chopped cucumbers while Sr. Corita washed a crate of lettuce in the sink in the kitchen of their home on Southwest Trafficway.

"Where's the garlic?" Sr. Berta said. "It was right here. I know I had it."

She started riffling through the onions, spices, and lettuce leaves that cluttered the countertop. Packages of pasta were piled on the floor, and every burner on the stove had a simmering pot filled with chili. Aluminum tins filled with already-made chili covered the kitchen table.

The year of 1981 had not started well. The center's caterers ceased operations for a tax problem, according to the sisters. Daycare requirements mandated that the children get a hot lunch. So, overnight, the sisters had to start up their own, illegal, catering operation.

As they carried in crates of lettuce, cucumbers, and tomatoes, cases of milk, drum-size canned goods, and doghouse-size boxes of cereal, their neighbors must have suspected they were operating a soup kitchen.

The sisters got up at 4:00 a.m. to make tacos, meatloaf, spaghetti, or chili for the 250 children. Then they transported the food to the school and placed it on a steam table that, mercifully, the caterers had left behind. The sisters added canned vegetables like corn and green beans, which they stored at the center.

They quickly became proficient at the quantities necessary to feed 250 children. It took 70 pounds of ground beef to make hamburgers, for example. Every pot they owned was in service five days a week on their four-burner stove. It took hours to make enough chili, and they used everything from saucepans to soup pots.

In addition to finding a caterer, the sisters now had to find a new location for the school and daycare. They had stalled their landlord at 4825 Troost for as long as possible, and they feared the police would show up to evict them.

After school hours, the sisters drove around looking for a new location. During the school year, space was at a premium, and nothing met the requirements of being both workable and affordable.

HELTER-SKELTER SHELTER

Finally, in April 1981, the sisters found temporary space to house the daycare at Holy Temple Homes at 5100 Leeds Trafficway. The space included a large classroom, laundry room, and most of an upper floor. It had restrooms and janitorial facilities that the daycare would share with Holy Temple, which kept its offices in the building. The space was large enough to get a license for 43 children ages six weeks to six years, with no more than 24 under two years old.

The center signed a one-month lease on April 23 for $850, with an option to continue on a month-by-month basis. Not long after, Boone Elementary School at 8817 Wornall offered the group the use of several classrooms to house the kindergarten and school-age children.

Sr. Corita notified the Missouri Department of Health & Senior Services that, effective April 27, 1981, Catherine Gleaton would direct the nursery site at Holy Temple, and Sr. Berta would direct the childcare center at Boone Elementary.

Sr. Berta was also the bus driver, so now she had to get the children to two locations that were 10 miles apart in the center's 1974 International school bus. First, they used the bus to move all the tables, desks, chairs, and supplies to their respective new locations. Alas, it wasn't big enough, nor was the volunteer power strong enough, to move the playground equipment.

This became a sore point with UMKC, the new owners of 4825 Troost. A letter dated June 18, 1981, to Sr. Corita, said:

…As I stated yesterday, our contractor is in a position where he will have to delay our construction project unless this equipment is removed. Obviously, we cannot afford to have a construction delay; therefore, it will be necessary for you to have removed from this property by noon on Tuesday, June 23, 1981…. Any equipment remaining on this site at that time will be considered as not being of interest to you and our contractor will proceed with the cleaning out of this area.

> *I was in awe of Sr. Berta's ability to keep so many balls in the air.*
>
> **—Kim Davis, former employee**

We are sure you understand the situation we are in and hope this does not cause you any great inconvenience.
Thanking you for your time, I am,
Yours very truly,
Gerald D. Jensen
Assistant Vice Chancellor for Administrative Affairs

Moving a 20-foot-high jungle gym, playground equipment, and 250 tons of sand to another temporary location was more than even the sisters could handle.

"Tell him we'll put it on our to-do list," Sr. Berta said. Eventually, the sisters rented a truck and moved the jungle gym, slides, swings, and rolling barrels to the Holy Temple location. They left the sand behind.

GOING IN CIRCLES

The sisters were still cooking for 250 children, but now they had to deliver it to two separate locations. They were also doing laundry for the infants. So they would load up the bus with meals at 3617 Southwest Trafficway, then pick up the children—most of whom still lived around 31st and Flora—and drive the younger children to 5100 Leeds Trafficway. There, Sr. Berta unloaded the food and picked up the dirty laundry. The next stop was 8817 Wornall Road. The loop, which she repeated every day, was about 30 miles and took just under an hour, without traffic.

"You look beat," Sr. Corita observed when Sr. Berta returned from hauling a hamper of dirty diapers into the house in July 1981.

"I don't know how much longer I can do this," Sr. Berta said. Although they never expressed their reservations to the staff or the mothers whose lives they knew were so much tougher than theirs, the sisters did worry about not having the stamina for the job. They were both well into their 40s, and taking care of their own health was at the bottom of their priority lists. Sr. Corita chain-smoked Virginia Slims Menthol Lights,

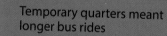
Temporary quarters meant longer bus rides

Temple that once occupied the Operation Breakthrough site

and Sr. Berta lived on burgers, fries, and chicken wings. They were lucky to get four hours of sleep a night.

"We have no real home, no hope of one, and no money to pay for one," Sr. Berta said. "We are in worse shape than when we started. The center is as homeless as some of the kids."

"Let's drive to Des Moines this weekend to visit my family," Sr. Corita said brightly, trying to cheer her up.

"Do you feel like what we are doing is right?" Sr. Corita asked, looking out across the horizon in southern Iowa. "I do. When you are convinced that something is right, you should keep doing it."

A LIKELY STORY

Sr. Berta returned ready to soldier on, determined to find a real home for Operation Breakthrough. After landlords had now evicted the center from two locations, she wanted to give the children a place that would endure.

Sr. Berta and Rich Koch started walking their former neighborhood, looking for possible locations. They saw signs of life. They learned that the Society of Saint Pius X had purchased the St. Vincent's church from Bishop Arvenus Penn in 1980.

According to Louis Tofari, author and historian, the diocese had refused to sell the church to the SSPX, which seeks to return to a pre-Vatican model, where priests conduct Mass in Latin. So the congregation approached Bishop Penn to act as a straw buyer. He bought the church for $65,000 and sold it to the SSPX congregation on the courthouse steps.

"It was a magnificent coup," Louis said. "The church cost $230,000 to build in 1924."

Rich and Sr. Berta trudged on, heading east. At 10 in the morning, a policeman approached the two on Prospect Avenue.

What are you two doing here?" he asked. The area was known for having many drug dealers.

"We're looking for a place to move our school," Berta said.

"A likely story," the cop snorted. "Do you have identification?"

"I'm Sr. Berta," she replied.

"A likely story."

They went from one downtrodden building to another. The two began to feel like building inspectors. They saw rats, refuse, and signs of squatters. Sr. Berta shook her head.

"Imagine, in a city with such wealth, people having to live like this."

A TREE GROWS IN BUILDING

When a Realtor told Rich and Sr. Berta about a building for sale at 3039 Troost for $180,000, they didn't expect much. The building had been a freestanding J.C. Penney store on a 33,315-square-foot tract of land that had once been part of a plantation with slaves. The store had both a two-story section and a one-story section, with a full basement and 18,400 square feet of retail space. In its mid-20th-century heyday, 31st and Troost was a robust retail district with a Jones Store, Florsheim Shoe Store, Western Auto, Woolworth's, Katz Drugstore, and Isis Theatre. In the 1920s, Walt Disney opened a studio there, where he created Mickey Mouse.

J.C. Penney had torn down the Second Church of Christ Scientist in 1955 to erect the store. Designed by New York architect F.R. Comstock, the church had been a majestic, Roman-Doric temple of white Phoenix stone and 44-foot-high columns that bore more than a passing resemblance to the Pantheon in Rome. It opened on Christmas day in 1904.

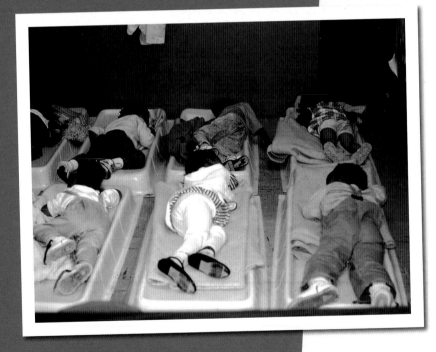

For 51 years, the church ministered to its flock until the department store acquired the property and tore it down. As a temple of retail, the building didn't last quite as long.

By the time Rich and Sr. Berta stood in front of it, a tree poked through its roof. The plywood boarding up the windows had grayed and rotted. Garbage and graffiti were everywhere. But Sr. Berta thought the place had potential.

U.S. Life Real Estate Services now owned the building. The Realtor said they would need a down payment of at least $30,000, which, of course, they didn't have. Maybe Joanne Collins, the city council representative from the district, could help. Sr. Berta says:

Her response was, "I don't think that's a very good idea. It's a high-crime area. There are prostitutes and drug dealers hanging out at this intersection. Children wouldn't be safe here."

I told her there are two major bus lines that pass through this intersection. Transportation is a huge barrier for our families. Besides, the crime isn't any higher than where these kids already live.

The councilwoman said, "Over my dead body would children move into this building."

RISKY BUSINESS

Sr. Corita called an emergency board meeting. She explained that the center's Title XX funds could be used to rent, but not to buy, space. Money would have to come from somewhere else.

"Wow, taking that kind of risk is huge," Rich advised. "The purchase could also be quite complicated." Rich had taken a job in public accounting with Arthur Anderson and then moved to Fox & Company.

"We need a home," Sr. Berta said.

"There might be a way," Rich said.

Rich talked to his wife, Kathy, about forming a corporation to purchase the building, which they would then rent to Operation Breakthrough.

"Srs. Berta and Corita are family," Kathy said. "They have been like grandparents to our children. Let's do it."

The Kochs formed K&R Properties, Inc., to purchase the building. Operation Breakthrough would pay enough rent for the company to pay the mortgage.

Rich called his parents in Uniondale, New York, to ask if they would be willing to lend Operation Breakthrough $30,000 for a down payment. They had heard their son's stories over the years and agreed to help.

Sr. Corita signed a promissory note in the summer of 1981 to pay Joseph J. Koch and Mary V. Koch "the sum of $30,000 dollars together with interest at the rate of 20 percent per annum on the deferred balances until paid. Said principal and interest shall be paid in 96 installments of not less than $628.60 each…"

K&R Properties, Inc., guaranteed the note.

The day the sisters got the keys to the building, they were giddy with the possibilities. As they headed toward the building, they talked about someday building a pool there. They opened the door of the center's new home…and found rain pouring in through the roof. Sr. Berta says:

We were deep in debt and needed help to fix the roof and renovate the building. I asked the city if there were any funds. James Threatt, who was now the assistant city manager, told us that before the city could give us funds to renovate, he would have to conduct a thorough study to determine the likelihood of us being around for another 10 years. He paid a consultant $10,000 for the study, which concluded it was unlikely the organization would survive.

I would have told him that for free.

Outing to Freedom Fountain in Kansas City

CHAPTER 13

DOWN AND OUT

Sitting at her desk, Sr. Berta shook her head and turned to Sr. Corita at a desk nearby. "I didn't get a minute of sleep last night worrying about how we are going to pay the mortgage."

"And did all that worrying produce any money?" queried Sr. Corita, with the steely calm of a black-jack dealer.

Operation Breakthrough now had its own home, but security came at a price. The center had to make a $628.60 payment to Rich's parents every month, plus a payment of about $1,800 to U.S. Life, which had agreed to finance the remaining $150,000.

"We didn't know if we'd be able to make the first payment," says Sr. Corita. "We had to get a loan from Laurel Bank for $500 to buy strippers, wax, and cleaning supplies." The staff came in on a Saturday to scrub down the building. There were several men loitering at the intersection who agreed to help.

"They were just like angels from heaven," Sr. Corita says.

The kids aged two and above moved into the building first. The only work required for licensing

The sisters hid the dire circumstances from the children

was to install fire alarms and fence in a playground. After classes at Boone Elementary School on August 12, 1981, the sisters, staff, a few volunteers, and some of the older children began loading desks, tables, books, and supplies on the school bus and moving them to 3039 Troost.

The doors opened at 6:00 a.m. on Monday, August 15. Volunteers from AT&T had constructed half-height walls to divide the open spaces. They were the only separation between the areas for the toddlers and preschool-age children. The dividers contained the bodies but not the voices. The sounds were more thunderous than a KISS concert, and the rock band relied on amplifiers to reach eardrum-splitting levels.

The classes for the school-age children were on the lower level, so they had some relief from the noise.

The babies up to two years old needed partitions, running water, and a kitchen. So they stayed at Holy Temple for the first few months, while renovations were under way. The Community Development office of Kansas City contributed $130,000 for renovations, and the U.S. Department of Agriculture contributed $63,000 to outfit a kitchen.

UNITED THEY STOOD ON SHAKY GROUND

In late fall, the center got a license for 250 children from six weeks to 12 years of age. The babies came to the center in February 1982, marking the first time Operation Breakthrough controlled its own destiny under one roof…albeit a leaky one.

The center had raised the money to build a kitchen, but not to hire a cook. At 6:00 a.m. on Monday before the infants arrived, Sr. Berta, Sr. Corita, and Mae Richardson arrived to cook breakfast and lunch.

The sisters marveled at their good fortune. Their new kitchen had a huge stove, big pans, and a walk-in freezer. Only a few months ago, they had been making chili in saucepans at home. They could do in an hour what used to take all night. They felt like Julia Child in the kitchens of Le Cordon Bleu.

"Can you believe how easy this is?" Sr. Berta said. "And we don't have to cart it all over Kansas City."

For the first few years, the center managed to stay afloat. Employees were always patient when their payroll checks bounced.

I thought I'd landed in the jaws of hell on my first day on the job. It sounded like Arrowhead Stadium would if the Chiefs won a Super Bowl.

—Kim Davis, former employee

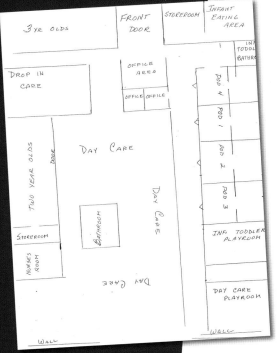

3039 Troost floorplan

A few even went into their own pockets to pay a bill here and there. However, the center was growing, and keeping up with the expenses began to take its toll, especially because the growth didn't come with an increase in funding.

By 1985, resources had thinned. By 1986, they broke. The organization had 58 employees, up from only 24 employees in 1982. The city had granted an application to increase capacity. The 1984 license allowed for 247 children from ages 6 weeks to 12 years, with no more than 48 under age 2.

The Missouri Division of Family Services had made subsidy cuts and spending freezes that forced Operation Breakthrough to limit attendance. More than 500 children were on the center's waiting list, Sr. Corita says.

"The division's fiscal irresponsibility, constant policy changes, lack of direction and communication will, in the very near future, result in the loss of safe, quality childcare facilities for working parents," she said in an article by Rick Alm in *The Kansas City Star* in early 1986.

"We didn't have any money," Sr. Berta says. "Bouncing paychecks wasn't so unusual, but now our checks to suppliers were also bouncing."

Srs. Corita and Berta went over every bill and asked themselves, *Which ones do we have to pay?* The annual bill for diapers alone was almost $15,000. Rich's parents always got their check, but the sisters weren't above playing games with U.S. Life.

A KITE THAT DIDN'T FLY

The monthly mortgage check to U.S. Life kept getting mailed later and later in the month. A few didn't get mailed at all. A representative from the company started calling regularly. Sr. Berta says:

I promised to mail him a check for $1,800, but I knew it would bounce. So I put the check in an envelope and

Sr. Berta discovered the numbers didn't add up

addressed it to "Dallas, California." After a few days, the guy called to ask where his check was.

I told him that I'd mailed it several days ago.

"I'm tired of your stories," he said.

"It's true."

"I don't believe you."

During this time, I got a call from an insurance company. I had been in a car accident. Someone had pulled out from a driveway and broadsided our car. The driver claimed his artificial leg slipped off the brake to the gas pedal. The accident injured my leg.

The insurance company had called several times to settle the case. I yelled to Corita, "How much do we need to pay people on Monday and send a check that won't bounce to the real Dallas?"

"We need at least $6,000," she replied. I told the claims adjuster I would settle for $6,000, under the condition that we got the check by Monday.

The envelope came back several days later, stamped "undeliverable." Then I put the check in another envelope and mailed it to Dallas, Texas, because I knew it would clear now.

The cycle soon repeated. When U.S. Life didn't get its mortgage checks for a couple of months, it threatened to foreclose on the property.

Rich called the accounts receivable department and said, "You do not want to foreclose on two nuns and put several hundred inner-city kids onto the street. This would be the worst public relations disaster in the history of the company."

Apparently, the young functionary agreed with this reasoning because he delivered Rich's threat to an executive of the company who called Rich several days later to thank him for averting an embarrassing situation.

This kept the leaky roof over Operation Breakthrough, but it did not solve the cash-flow problems.

The sisters couldn't say no to the children or their parents

SCHOOL'S OUT

Sr. Berta didn't care much about clothes. She would grab a sweater from a pile, don gray knitted jogging pants, and call herself dressed. Her clothes looked like they came from the clearance rack at thrift stores. She took much ribbing about her "rag bag" look. Suddenly, she started coming to work in neatly pressed shirts and the occasional jacket. The staff knew this had nothing to do with turning over a new fashion leaf.

"Oooooh," said Mae Richardson from her perch at the front desk. "Sr. Berta's got her pimping clothes on today." The staff knew she would be calling on someone, hoping for a donation.

It pained her to ask anyone for money, so instead she talked to people about her dreams for the children. And they were as vast as the needs.

The sisters looked for other ways to lower expenses. The options got more painful.

"We have to make some hard choices," Sr. Corita said. "Do we close part of the school or the childcare center?" They called a meeting of the board. Over the years, the number of children attending the upper grades had declined, while the demand for childcare grew. The board voted to cease offering classes for grades four to eight in 1984.

This decision did little to allay the financial difficulties, however. In 1986, the sisters called another meeting to discuss disbanding the rest of the grade levels, from kindergarten to third grade. In 1985, a federal district judge, Russell Clark, ruled that racial segregation, dilapidated schools, and poorly performing students needed remedies. He ordered the state and district to spend almost $2 billion to build new schools, integrate classrooms, and bring test scores up to national norms.

Even on the darkest days, the children brought joy

"With all the money, students in these grades should have more options and better facilities in public schools," Sr. Corita said. "That isn't true for affordable childcare. The need for childcare is too overwhelming, and we could use more space for the younger children."

"Corita, think about the fashion shows and science projects from the school. How can we give that up?" Sr. Berta countered. "Remember the fifth-grade boy who got kicked out of public school because he couldn't read? After a year at our school, we'd see him coming out of the library with armloads of books."

"We can't keep going like this," Sr. Corita told her. "We don't have the resources. We have to prioritize."

"Isn't there something we could do to keep the classrooms?" said Sr. Berta, who seemed to regard prioritizing as offensive as stealing bread from babies.

"Just because this won't be an official school doesn't mean we won't keep trying to teach children," Sr. Corita said.

The board voted to cease offering classes for children older than six years old. Operation Breakthrough would confine itself to providing childcare for infants and preschoolers.

"This is our darkest hour," Sr. Berta said to Sr. Corita later that night.

Still, closing the school would not be enough to pay the mortgage, the utility bills, and the payroll. The situation grew so dire the sisters crossed the line of the law. They had done so in the past unwittingly. Now they knew what they were doing.

How do you dole out money when you have unlimited problems and finite resources? Sr. Berta won't answer that question.

—David Kierst, retired juvenile court commissioner

IRS INTEREST

Sr. Corita, who was in charge of the bookkeeping and human resources, stopped deducting the withholding taxes from employee salaries. By 1986, the center owed thousands in back taxes. The IRS started sending letters that calculated an amount that, with interest and penalties, was growing faster than kudzu.

Sr. Berta called Steve Osborne for help. Steve, who had worked with Rich at Fox & Company CPAs, had started his own firm in 1983. Steve says:

They were down about $100,000 in payroll taxes. That's a huge amount for anybody, but for an organization this size, it was monumental. The center needed to make catch-up payments with steep interest and still make current payments too. You don't want to use the IRS as your banker. This was a hopeless position.

Steve advised the sisters to pay the current amount due to avoid more penalties and show some intention to make good on the back taxes, for starters. He also gave them suggestions on how to negotiate a favorable deal. Sr. Corita made an appointment to meet with the IRS agent on the case.

The morning of the interview, Sr. Berta said to Sr. Corita, "This calls for desperate measures." The mischief in her smile telegraphed what she had in mind.

"Okay, let's dust off our habits," Sr. Corita agreed. They had to rummage around in the massive, leather steamer trunks now in their garage to take out the uniforms they had not worn since they had solicited bankers and begged the IRS to grant the center nonprofit status. The black-serge habits scratched, the white collar pinched, and the squared, white caps and hoods made them feel like mummies.

En route to the IRS, Sr. Berta said, "Corita, I don't think we are going to make it."

This time, Sr. Corita didn't dismiss her friend's assessment as the dire predictions of a worrywart or reassure her that God would provide for them.

"It may be time to fold," she said. This time, Sr. Berta didn't try to argue the point.

ARTFUL TAX DODGERS

With the closest approximation of saintly miens they could muster, Srs. Berta and Corita entered the sprawling IRS offices at 5800 E. Bannister Road in Kansas City. They had only a few minutes to talk their way out of $100,000 in back taxes.

Their agent looked at the handwritten budgets and their payment plan. He asked several questions before spelling out the situation.

Sr. Berta tried not to roll her eyes at the impossibility of ever paying back a sum so large. He said he would review the materials and get back to them. She was sure a jail term was in her future.

"We'll have to tell the staff about this," said Sr. Corita, as they walked slowly to their car. "We'll have to help them find other jobs."

"No, no, no, we can't let this happen," said Mae Richardson when Sr. Corita told the group gathered in the lunch room that the center would have to shut down. Several teachers burst into tears.

No one noticed that Helen Gragg wasn't wailing like the rest. She even had a faint smile on her face.

Field trip to Deanna Rose Farmstead

CHAPTER 14

IN MYSTERIOUS WAYS

Helen and John Gragg

Helen Gragg had almost paid off her house at 32nd and Euclid. She and her husband, John, had always lived within their means. When he passed away, John left her with a small pension. When she heard about the IRS troubles at Operation Breakthrough, she called her bank and asked if she could take out a second mortgage on her home. The bank agreed to lend her $30,000.

The next day, Helen went into Sr. Corita's office and looked to make sure no one else was around. The half-height walls separating the offices didn't afford much privacy. At first, Sr. Corita thought she had some personal or personnel problem to discuss, and groaned inwardly. However, Helen didn't sit down. She pulled an envelope out of her purse that read, "For Operation Breakthrough" and set it on the desk.

When Sr. Corita saw the check for $30,000, she let out one of her big, husky laughs that sounded like a balky car ignition starting.

"You can't do this for us," Sr. Corita said. "But you can do it for the children." As soon as Helen left, Sr. Corita called to her friend, "You are not going to believe this."

Sr. Berta was, for the first time her friend could remember, speechless.

Sr. Corita called the accountant, Steve Osborne. He marveled at the act:

This woman has no assurance she will ever get the money back or even get paid for her work. Yet she was willing to not just take money out of the bank but also to borrow the money to pay her employer. How many employees would be willing to take this risk? That shows how committed the employees were to the mission of the center.

With the $30,000, the sisters were able to negotiate a payment plan with the IRS. Helen's selfless act seemed to usher in a new era for Operation Breakthrough, as an ever wider net of people stepped forward to help.

FRONT-PAGE NEWS

A tall, slender, doe-eyed, young reporter grabbed her spiral notebook and headed for Operation Breakthrough in May 1989. Jennifer Howe hoped the sisters would make a nice, heartwarming, 800-word feature. It turned into a 3,000-word article that ran on June 24.

"Sisters of the Children" made the center come alive for thousands of Kansas Citians who had never heard of it before. The article began:

The two nuns stood at the curb at 31st Street and Troost Avenue, strapping babies into car seats as they do every weekday at 6:00 p.m.

"Who's this?" Sr. Berta asked, plucking a little boy out of a group of older children waiting to get into the van that would take them home from St. Vincent's Child-care Center. "You don't belong here." She hugged the child and sent him back inside the center.

"Does somebody in this van have dirty pants?" Sr. Berta asked. The older children giggled.

"You've got nine kids in there," Sr. Corita said.

"I counted eight—Oh, Lord," Sr. Berta said, quickly peering back inside.

Jennifer captured the chaos, the compassion, and the charm in abundance. One local TV news show did a follow-up story, then another. More Kansas Citians began sending checks, donating goods, and stopping by the center to unload a truck, rock a baby, or read to a child. Donations that used to come in single-digit numbers quintupled. James Hale, the newspaper's publisher, gave $20,000 to the center. Cheryl Womack donated $25,000, and the company she founded, VCW, adopted the center as a community service project. Jim Brady, from the Brady Center to Prevent Gun Violence in Washington, DC, paid a visit.

On December 27, 1989, the center got a belated Christmas gift from the scrawny kid whom Sr. Corita had recruited from a basketball court 20 years before. Kathy and Rich Koch dissolved K&R Properties and deeded the building to Operation Breakthrough. The price was "Ten Dollars and other good and valuable consideration."

"It was like winning the lottery," says Sr. Berta.

The good fortune seemed to replicate itself. Help came in many forms—dollars, expertise, sweat equity, and employees who never said, "That's not my job."

You can't help a child unless you help the family.

—Sr. Berta

The Kansas City Star would go on to publish 774 more stories that included the center over the years.

One of CEO Sr. Corita's favorite tasks

We did whatever we had to do to keep things running. We gave breathing treatments, shots, and medicine whether we were teachers, janitors, cooks, or nurses.

—**Patricia Thompson, facility manager**

Pat Thompson

JUST 20 HOURS A WEEK

Jennifer started volunteering at the center after work. At first, she wrote thank-you notes to the donors. Then she started helping with events. She joined the board of directors. She also married David Heinemann and had a child, then quit her newspaper job. After three weeks at home, Sr. Berta called.

"I know that baby of yours takes a nap in the afternoons," she said. "Why don't you come to work here just 20 hours a week?" Jennifer joined the staff in 2000. Her two sons spent their childhoods at the center.

A few volunteers wound up as employees. Patricia Thompson took a child development class after graduating high school in 1982. The class included an internship at Operation Breakthrough. Sr. Corita offered her a job as a teacher. When her family moved to Holden, Missouri, in 1996, she made the 130-mile round trip to the center for 15 years before moving back to Kansas City. Since 2010, she has been serving as the facility manager.

Lee Duckett began coming a few hours a week in 1998 to hand out gifts for 2,300 children through the Christmas warehouse. Since she had a background in desktop publishing, she offered to sort out the donor database, then agreed to head the Christmas effort the following year. In 2004, the Kansas City Chiefs selected Operation Breakthrough as the beneficiary of its next Chiefs Charity Game, and Sr. Berta suggested Lee become an employee.

"You could work just 20 hours a week to coordinate the effort."

"Ha!" Lee says. "It turned out to be 60 hours a week." Time commitments were as inexact as job descriptions at the center. Lee says:

One night someone brought a guinea pig. Sr. Berta sent me to buy a cage and food. The next day my assignment was to measure children for harnesses to meet a Headstart requirement.

Jennifer and David Heinemann with their first son

Michelle (left) and Lee Duckett

Then I served on the sandwich brigade, making 500 sandwiches to feed kids on a field trip and put kids in costumes for Halloween.

I started driving Sr. Berta to abandoned houses to look for moms who didn't bring their kids to the center. She is fearless. One day, I took her to a house where a guy had beaten up his girlfriend. I was nervous and not paying attention to how fast I was going. When a policeman pulled me over, Sr. Berta said, "Officer, I am a nun. If I promise to rap her knuckles with a ruler, would you let her off with just a warning?"

Once Operation Breakthrough catches someone in its vortex, it's hard to leave. Twenty-one of the most long-standing employees have amassed a collective total of 576 years of employment—an average of 27 years each. Those who leave often stay connected to the center.

Kim Davis came to Operation Breakthrough in 1992 to do a practicum before getting her master's degree in social work. She remembers the eye-opening expedition to the Stand for Children rally in Washington, DC, on June 1, 1996. Kim says:

Sr. Berta thought it would be a chance for the center's moms and kids to see the nation's capital and enjoy a road trip. She organized two buses with a group of about 130. We joined more than 300,000 people to hear presenters like Rosa Parks and Marian Wright Edelman.

Our group ranged in age from 93-year-old Grandma Ellis to a six-month-old infant. We couldn't see anything, and we kept losing people. It was so hot. The humidity reached 90 percent. There were lines for everything.

We got back on the bus that night and drove back. What struck me was how few of the moms had ever been out of Kansas City. They were excited to pass through each new state. All I could think of was getting home. For me, this was the trip from hell. For the moms, this was a great adventure.

Then one mom said, "This is the nicest vacation I've ever had." It made me realize how small some of their worlds were.

Kim became the center's director of social services.

Kim Davis left in 2011 to become the executive director of Amethyst Place, which helps women recovering from addictions. It partners with Operation Breakthrough.

Chiefs Charity Games were a godsend to the center

Christine Sill-Rogers served for more than a decade on the Operation Breakthrough board and became a circuit court judge.

Since 1997, the Foundation for Lawyers Encouraging Academic Performance (LEAP) has raised more than $1.2 million for the center.

Sr. Berta met Hillary Clinton during her 1997 visit to Kansas City

MAGNETIC FIELD

It became a standing joke that all Sr. Berta had to do was say she needed something and someone would step forward to provide it.

"I sure wish we had a nurse," she said one afternoon in 1995. The same day, William Jewell College called to offer one. Next it was a social worker. Everything from Halloween costumes and car seats to a medical clinic and mortgage payments seemed to materialize as soon as Sr. Berta expressed a need.

One day she was looking for a car seat to give a new mom. "Surely we have one around here," she said. At that moment, a woman drove up with five of them to donate in her trunk.

One year, the center needed gifts for hundreds of children. Sherri and Tom Waris came through the door with armloads full. Their children helped with the Christmas warehouse.

Christine Sill-Rogers worked at a large law firm that handled pro-bono cases, most in the juvenile division. She started helping Sr. Berta in 1990 with a boy who was running away from school. Her next case was helping Sam, a teenager, whose girlfriend had killed their newborn baby. The courts wanted to take away his three-year-old daughter, but Sam wanted to raise her. She helped him get the support he needed to take care of his daughter.

Two prominent Kansas City attorneys, Linda French and Jack Kilroy, got together in 1994 to start a charitable organization to help improve the public's opinion of lawyers. The Foundation for Lawyers Encouraging Academic Performance (LEAP) brought together representatives from area bar associations.

Claudia York, who had graduated from law school, handled the pro-bono work at Shugart Thompson & Kilroy. When Jack asked her to suggest beneficiaries, she said, "Kids!"

In LEAP's second year, the board visited Operation Breakthrough and soon adopted the center.

Attorney Steve Millin, known now as Saint Steve around Operation Breakthrough, got off to a bumpy start with Sr. Berta. He was set to present her with a check for $500 at a breakfast meeting of LEAP. He was a little miffed when she didn't show up at the appointed time. Then she called to apologize. She'd had to find a place for three children who were living in a car after their mother died of AIDs. He says:

When I gave her the check, she said it would be used to buy footlockers. When I smiled, she said, "You don't think that is important, do you? A lot of our kids are in foster care. They go from home to home every 30 days with their few possessions in black trash bags," she said. "We're going to give them their own personal trunks with stencils and markers that they can make their own. Now, when they go to a new home, it will be with the dignity of carrying their own luggage, not a trash bag."

I was crying that day—thinking about children in our city wandering around with black trash bags, not knowing what tomorrow would bring.

I've been a disciple ever since. I will represent any person Sr. Berta asks me to help. My two guiding rules are: When Sr. Berta asks, I do it, and I don't ask why.

In 1995, Senia and Will Shields, an offensive guard for the Kansas City Chiefs, funded a literacy program through their Will to Succeed Foundation. It was just the beginning of their generosity. (In 2009, the Will to Succeed Foundation paid off the center's $405,000 mortgage.) They would bring in other players and even the coach and his wife.

In 1997, Haver Danner, the owner of Mail Print, donated a bag of diapers in response to a newspaper story. He told Sr. Corita that if she ever needed any printing to let him know. Since then, the company—now called NextPage—has printed every business card, invitation, and brochure that Operation Breakthrough

has produced…without submitting a bill. The sisters made another friend the same year: Hillary Clinton, who visited with them during a trip to Kansas City.

In 2000, soon after Dick Vermeil came to coach the Kansas City Chiefs, his wife, Carol, volunteered at Operation Breakthrough. She rocked babies, changed diapers, and took a personal interest in the welfare of her charges. She and Dick helped influence the Chiefs to make Operation Breakthrough the beneficiary of its annual Charity Game from 2005 to 2008. The games raised more than $2 million for the center. (Founded in 1984, the Kansas City Chiefs Charity Game is the most successful and longest-running benefit game in the National Football League.)

"There is a magnetic field around Operation Breakthrough," Cecelia Sevart says.

Almost every weekend for the last several years, Scott Burnett, a Jackson County legislator from the 1st District, dons old jeans and a t-shirt and drives the Operation Breakthrough box truck around the metro to pick up donated furniture and deliver it to the center's warehouse.

In 2014, the International Design Guild chose Operation Breakthrough for a $25,000 makeover. Over the course of a week, volunteers turned a dark, cluttered warren into an airy space that became "2 Sisters Park" with a mushroom table, green ball chairs, and bookshelves. The effort also created a parent resource center with computers for job searches and rooms for giving away clothing and household goods.

Sr. Berta is the most charismatic person I have ever met.

—Steve Millin, volunteer

The center is like quicksand. Once you stand in it, it's hard to leave.

—Cecelia Sevart, former employee

Former Kansas City Chiefs coach Dick Vermeil with Sr. Corita

The center's clinic now has two physicians, two pediatric nurse practitioners, nurses, and support staff.

SAY "AHHH"

Children's Mercy Hospital offered to staff a nurse at Operation Breakthrough in February 1996.

"I hear you got money for a nurse," said Maria Little, RN, to Sr. Berta on a Thursday. She had volunteered at the center for a few years helping with physicals.

"Do you want the job?" was the reply. That was the interview. Maria started work the following Monday. She carved out 100 square feet of space from a storeroom in the basement, where the employees office. She had a desk, a computer, a stethoscope, an instrument kit, and a sink, which she shared with everyone else in the building. By 1998, Maria, who became a pediatric nurse practitioner (PNP), had convinced Children's Mercy to open an offsite clinic at Operation Breakthrough.

Harriet Navarre, PNP, started working full-time at Operation Breakthrough in August 1998. The two women treated and diagnosed everything from colds and asthma to abuse and neglect; they splinted fingers and administered antibiotics for infections. They visited every classroom daily to detect problems before they became emergencies.

Kevin Cummings was a dental student when he and his wife, Mary, a nursing student, started sending their children to Operation Breakthrough in the 1980s. The center helped them get through school. "Someday I'll pay you back," he used to say to the sisters. Then one day in the late 1990s, he showed up and said, "I'm ready."

He solicited area companies like H&R Block to donate money for top-notch equipment, including two dental chairs and an X-ray machine. Working alongside volunteer and former student Shelby Payne, he helped build the dental clinic. Kevin brought his staff down to the center once a week to see 40 to 50 kids a day.

Most of the center's employees are also volunteers. They come after hours and work off the clock to help with events. Two long-time employees, Sister Elizabeth Seaman and Sister Theresa Kramps, often babysat children, bought them birthday presents, and regularly donated their modest salaries for the children's welfare.

These are just a small sampling of the largesse Operation Breakthrough has attracted.

Harriett Navarre, Maria Little, and Angela McFadden at the Children's Mercy Hospital clinic at the center

A FLOOD OF PUBLICITY

Sometimes even bad news turned into good. In 2004, the city tore down three dilapidated apartment buildings. The crews closed off a sewer line they assumed was inactive.

Early on Monday, November 29, the first staff members showed up at Operation Breakthrough after the Thanksgiving break to discover that six inches of water had flooded the basement. They grabbed brooms and tried to knock sparking electrical plugs out of their sockets while standing in water. The flood ruined carpets, computers, and bags of donated clothing.

"This is so disheartening," Kim Davis said. "How do we even deal with this?" She turned to Sr. Berta and said, "You'll have to close the center today." The basement housed the administrative offices, the medical clinic, and the before- and after-school programs.

"Everyone will help; we can do this," Sr. Berta said. "Call the local TV stations." Then she dropped a doll in the water.

The staff spent the day using a single shop vacuum to suction out the water in the 16,000-square-foot space, which would've been like using a shot glass to bail out the Titanic. They used children's blocks to raise the desks and chairs so they could dry. The center was open for business on Monday, with few aware of the salvage operations taking place on the lower level.

That night, two TV stations featured the floating doll in their evening broadcasts. The stories inspired a flood of donations. Going forward, whenever the organization got into a bind, Sr. Berta would quip, "Why don't we flood the basement? Give me a garden hose."

The media coverage put the center on the radar at City Hall.

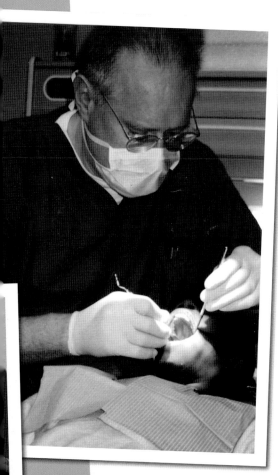

Kevin Cummings, DDS, donated the dental clinic

Will Shields, and his wife, Senia, through their Will to Succeed Foundation paid off the center's mortgage

PRETTY IN PINK

The mayor's office invited Operation Breakthrough to join a group of Kansas Citians who traveled to Anaheim, California, to accept the All-America City award in 2006. The city would pay for the flights and the hotel. Most of the kids, who ranged in age from five to 18 years old, had never been on a plane, stayed in a hotel room, left town, or even owned a suitcase.

Dawn Taylor, a volunteer, organized a luggage drive. Soon, suitcases in all shapes and sizes began arriving, including a complete set of vintage, pink, hard-sided suitcases with pink-polka-dot fabric lining.

"Our luggage was even more diverse than we were," says Sr. Berta.

The kids would perform a dance as part of a cultural competition, and they practiced their routines in the hotel lobby with adults from the Kansas City contingent. Among the group was LaShantese Ward. The once sad and hurt toddler had become a smiling, spunky kid under Connie Crumble's doting care. Connie still laughs about the day she took LaShantese for her first day at Gordon Parks Elementary School. When the new teacher stumbled over her name, the little girl promptly deployed the technique Connie had taught her. Accompanying each syllable of her name with a clap, she said, "It's La-Shan-Tese," then asked, "If you can't say my name, how can you teach me?"

LaShantese had diligently practiced her dance routine and couldn't wait to see Sr. Berta's face when they performed. "Sr. Berta glowed when we came in seventh place, out of hundreds," she says.

The group got to see Disneyland and go to the beach. Sr. Berta says:

These kids had never seen the ocean. One kicked up water and yelled, "Sr. Berta, look at me!" A local looked me up and down and asked, "Is that your brother? You sure are a strange-looking group."

Sr. Berta never stopped searching for new ways to provide children with adventures, whether on the road or at the home with Sr. Corita.

Kansas City Chiefs hosted NFL PLAY 60 clinics at the center

Kansas City Mayor Kay Barnes and civic leader Mike Burke on an All-America City trip to California

CHAPTER 15

SHE'S NOT A SAINT, SHE'S MY MOTHER

Vanshay with Sr. Corita

"Pass the corn," says four-year-old Leilani.

"What do you say?" prompts her father, Chris, age 27.

"Please?"

"That's good."

Chris was a fifth grader living with his five siblings in a Ford Tempo when his mother approached Sr. Berta for help. She enrolled the younger children at Operation Breakthrough and the older ones in public school. A relative took the younger children home. Chris had nowhere to go, so the sisters took him.

"I don't know what would have happened to me without the sisters," Chris says. "Waking up to Sr. Corita's French toast and bacon every morning—that was sweet. Those two sisters mean the world to me."

Now he has a daughter of his own. He was the victim of identity theft last year, which made it hard for him to get a job, so he and his daughter came back to live with the sisters. The two are part of a crowd of eight having dinner in the sisters' Raytown home.

The meal is buffet style and on paper plates, as usual. In the kitchen sit pots of spaghetti—one spicy, one not—oven-baked chicken, corn, salad, and garlic bread. The group dines at the biggest table in the house, an oak, oblong table in a dining room walled with smoked mirrors. With eight around the table, it's crowded, but pleasantly so, and the mirrored walls increase the effect.

"Tyrez, don't eat that chicken with your hands," Sr. Berta says. Tyrez, whom the sisters adopted as an infant, pauses to consider but then picks up the chicken with the quiet defiance typical of a 15-year-old. The sisters face a daily battle to rouse him for school. His favorite class is physics, but he refuses to spend time on subjects that don't interest him.

Ronnie

Resentful of Sr. Berta's interference in his life, he accuses her of being a "control freak."

"She calls me a lot…it seems like every five minutes," he says. "She wants to know…did you do your homework? Can you check to see if the mail arrived? Will you make sure the dogs don't get the TV remotes?

"She's a good leader, but she worries about everything," he continues. "She's afraid the dogs will get lost in the house or run away. I hope she's not afraid I'll run away."

"She's Attila the Nun," laughs Chris, pointing toward Sr. Berta.

"Where's Ronnie? He should be home by now," Sr. Berta says, unfazed by the epithet. "I'm going to call him." The 21-year-old is one of four children the sisters have adopted officially.

She pulls her smartphone from her cleavage, and Chris's phone rings. He sees the number and laughs, "Berta, you boob-dialed me again."

She dials Ronnie. He has stopped to pick up an order of meat from Mc-Gonigle's. He tells Sr. Berta, "When the woman behind the counter found out it was for you, she said, 'We should give her this for free. That woman is a saint.' I told her, 'Oh yeah? You should live with her.' "

Sr. Berta gets a big laugh when she repeats this to her kids. So does Leilani when she dips her nose in the whipped topping on the strawberry shortcake that Chris has assembled. She is trying to see how much she can eat without using her hands. Chris glares at her and shakes his head.

Nearby, Jaylin, a finicky eater, quietly makes his way through a mound of spaghetti. The 16-year-old, who's lived with the sisters off and on for years, is mercurial. He can go from pliant and affable to raging faster than a Porsche goes from zero to 60. This night, he is agreeable, if taciturn.

Vanshay, whom the sisters also adopted as an infant, gazes at her brother, Tyrez, with the cool dispassion of a 14-year-old. The pretty, sleepy-eyed eighth grader, still in her plaid skirt from Presentation School, tries to look like she is dining with strangers. Then Chris, who coaches the basketball team at her school, teases her about her game.

A radiant smile breaks through.

Sr. Berta announces to all, "Remember, it's Kenyauta's graduation on Thursday." She had been attending a program for disabled children.

"I've ordered the cake," says Donna Wike, as she feeds Kenyauta, or Yauty, who smiles from her wheelchair near the table. Donna has been a caregiver to the 21-year-old, and a de facto family member, for the last

The sisters were always raising someone else's children as their own. A whole trail of kids would follow them into work.

—Marilyn Driver, former teacher

seven years. Yauty cannot speak, hear, or leave her motorized wheelchair. The other diners periodically smile at her.

"Where's Myles?" says Sr. Berta. The 21-year-old drives all the kids to school before he goes to work.

"He's not feeling well," Vanshay says. "He's in the bathroom." The children giggle conspiratorially.

"Where's the salt?" Sr. Corita says, glaring at Sr. Berta, sure she has hidden it deliberately. And she has, ever trying to reduce Corita's blood pressure.

Sometimes, when Sr. Corita gets annoyed with Sr. Berta, she'll sit down at the piano in the entryway and bang out some Chopin, Tchaikovsky, or Mozart.

After a few more minutes of conversation, distractions pull each of them away. Chris and Tyrez excuse themselves. Jaylin and Vanshay dive into their iPhones.

Similar scripts play out at family dinners around the country, but the easy banter and sibling teasing mask more trauma than 100 families might experience. Yauty's mother was a drug addict and a prostitute. The mothers of Ronnie, Vanshay, and Tyrez were all too overwhelmed with the struggle to survive to take proper care of their children.

Of course, most children don't have parents who are also nuns in their 70s and 80s. The household is cluttered with mementos, artwork, photos, books, toys, and furniture from different epochs.

"It's a madhouse, bedlam, with clothes all over the floor," Sr. Corita says. "We have to be careful not to step on a sleeping body. We never know who might show up for a night or two." Adding to the chaos are three large dogs—two affable chocolate Labradors, Hershey and Cocoa, and Lady, a skittish shepherd mix.

"Berta tries to micromanage everything," Sr. Corita said to a dinner guest who had come to observe the family. "She wants everything perfect. With this many people in the house, that won't happen."

Tyrez as a young boy

BUMPY ROAD TO PARENTHOOD

Srs. Berta and Corita had been taking children home when their parents needed someone to look after them since their days at Our Lady of the Angels. Tony and Dorothy had been living there almost full-time since the early 1970s. Occasionally, a parent would get into trouble and ask the sisters to take their kids for a few days.

At the center, they saw the way the foster care system ravaged the lives of children, sending them from one home to another, sometimes every month and often with no warning.

"We thought if we became foster parents, we could help fix some of the problems," Sr. Berta says. "At least we could keep the kids in one place until they could go home to parents, a relative, or an adoptive home." They became official foster parents in March 1994. Sr. Berta says:

The social worker who assessed us asked if we would be willing to take a child in a wheelchair.

"No wheelchair, because we have steps," we told her.

"What about a child who was deaf?"

"Deaf, no, we don't know sign language."

"Will you take a blind child?"

"No, neither of us knows braille."

Kenyauta turned out to be incapable of walking, seeing, or hearing.

We thought if we worked hard enough, she would be all right. It's a journey people with disabled kids take. Eventually, we applied to adopt Kenyauta. The first social worker tried to convince us we were too old. We were in our mid-50s.

The judge spent about 30 minutes grilling us on our sexual orientation.

"Are you homosexual?" he wanted to know.

I told him, "No, but what difference would that make? Who is going to adopt this child?"

Kenyauta with Shominique

Berta and Corita are the closest thing to saints we will ever know. Their goodness resonates.

—Steve Millin, volunteer

Having children no more makes you a parent than having a piano makes you a pianist.

—Sr. Berta, quoting Michael Levine

Kenyauta's mother used cocaine during pregnancy, and her child tested positive for several other drugs. The infant stopped breathing and had several seizures during her first days of life. The sisters had to put her on a sleep apnea monitor at night. An alarm sounded every time Kenyauta stopped breathing for more than 10 seconds. The first night, it went off 16 times.

Soon, the sisters had three small children living with them at their home, then at 89th and Wornall Road. When the BVM order found out about the adoption, the mother superior called and told them, "Nuns don't adopt kids."

"Why not?" asked Sr. Berta.

"How are you going to support them?"

"We knew the BVMs would have a problem with this," Sr. Berta says. "So we didn't ask. We just did it. The order found out after the fact."

Kenyauta, who is now 21, has the mind of an 18-month-old child. She has never walked or spoken, other than to emit grunts and groans.

Soon after taking in Kenyauta, they took in Ronnie as a foster child. He also was born addicted. Ronnie had difficulty focusing, but his deficits were minimal.

A suitable couple came forward to adopt him when he was four. Ronnie broke out in hives, screamed, and shouted when they visited him. The couple backed out of the adoption, so the sisters adopted him.

Next came biological siblings Tyrez and Vanshay, who were babies when the sisters took them.

Over the years, the sisters have cared for more than 70 children, some as official fosters, some as houseguests of indeterminate duration. There are usually around seven or eight staying in the home at any given time, and there have been as many as 11.

Leilani with Vanshay

In 2015, in addition to Yauty, Chris, Myles, Ronnie, Tyrez, Vanshay, and Leilani, the household also included Nicholas and Cardell. Cardell studies engineering at college during the week but spends some weekends with the sisters.

Some have criticized the sisters for being too generous to their children. Sr. Berta especially is prone to making sure her kids have the newest Nike shoes and latest iPhones.

"She wants her children to have whatever they want," Lee Duckett says. "If they want an XBox, they get one."

Susie Roling, a former clinical case manager at the center, says:

She feels guilty that the kids are being raised by nuns. She isn't their biological mother. She isn't young enough. So she overcompensates by giving them things. I told her, "You are like Mother Teresa. Your children are lucky."

Sr. Berta, who often lamented that she didn't have a young mother when she was growing up, now does the same for her children, but she does her best to make up for what she perceives as shortcomings. She goes to their basketball and soccer games, enrolls them in camps, and rents them horses.

Sometimes, she outsources certain tasks to others.

THE BIRDS AND THE BEES

"I want you to talk to my younger kids about sex," Sr. Berta said to Susie. "They won't listen to an old nun talk about it."

"What do you want me to say to them about sex?" she asked with a smile.

"Encourage them to wait until they are older to have sex. Tell them you appreciate this might be hard. Tell them that if they don't wait, they have to use birth control. Tell them condoms are available."

Susie came to work at the center in 2004 as a family advocate after getting a degree in social work from Catholic University of America in Washington, DC. She had planned to become a nun but wasn't sure what order to join. At first, she had few dealings with Sr. Berta. Susie says:

Sr. Corita handled all the personnel. Sr. Berta didn't know my name for six months. She called me Margot, the name of another advocate with blond hair. I noticed her, though. Seeing how she lived the gospel of Jesus daily was the most inspiring thing I'd ever been around. She soon went from being my superior to being my dear friend.

Susie connected with Sr. Berta in a way few others did. The closeness of their relationship prompted Susie to explore joining the BVM order. When she learned that she would have to leave Kansas City to study, she became a lay member of the BVM community.

She is in some ways Berta's doppelganger, just as determined and devoted to social justice, but with a sunnier viewpoint. She has become quite involved in the lives of the sisters' adopted and foster children, and often steps in to do Sr. Berta's bidding. Susie says:

It is difficult to say no to her. Sr. Berta asked me if I would spend time with a 14-year-old girl who needed help…for a few days. Eventually, I took her home, and she became a permanent member of our family.

If Sister Berta had a house big enough for every homeless child, she would take them all home.

—Susie Roling, former employee

Sr. Berta would go to the moon and back to give her kids a happy childhood.

—Susie Roling

Tyrez

IN PARENTS' SHOES

As Sr. Berta's own children grow older, she sees it's not enough to give toddlers a boost. Their caretakers and families may need help. And the children may need services after they leave the center. The experience of being mothers has given the sisters more understanding and sympathy for what the parents of their students face. Sr. Berta says:

I've learned a lot by being a parent. Before we had kids, a mother told me, "My child isn't here today because we couldn't find his shoes." I remember thinking, *What kind of house do you live in if your child can't find his shoes?* Now I know. When one of my kids says he can't find his shoes, I tell him to find someone else's—there has to be a pair somewhere.

We had a woman living next door with a child. She went to work and tied her two-year-old to the bed. She left him with some books, a potty chair, and some food and went to work. When someone reported her, she said, "I had two choices. I could not work, and we would both be homeless, or I could do what I did." Being a parent yourself puts you more in touch with the real world.

Being parents also strengthened the sisters' attachment to the Operation Breakthrough kids for whom the real world is often a grim, joyless place. They were never content just to feed, clothe, and educate children. They wanted the children to catch a fish, see a play, ride a bike, pick a pumpkin, and listen to music.

Thanks to the generosity of Kansas Citians, the children have. They've gone to concerts, the circus, pumpkin patches, and the Nelson-Atkins Museum of Art. Twice a year, two musicians from the Kansas City Symphony perform at the center.

Although regulations now forbid chickens and boa constrictors, Sister Elizabeth Seaman brings her dog, Shadow, a Spaniel mix, to entertain the kids. And the Pets for Life group sends a golden retriever named Doc. Volunteers come every day to delight the children with stories, games, or art projects and help them with reading, homework, or using computers.

It is never enough for Sr. Berta, though.

Nuns with son Ronnie

Kenyauta with Sr. Corita

CHAPTER 16
A MA AND PA SHOP NO MORE

Photographer Gloria Baker Feinstein donated most of the portraits of children used in the last three chapters.

"I couldn't sleep last night, and I had a bright idea," Sr. Berta said to Lee Duckett, the center's associate director of marketing and events.

"Oh no," Lee groaned.

Sr. Berta has terrorized the staff regularly with these two sentences. They signal the intersection of insomnia and inspiration, two states with which she is intimately familiar and from which issue forth a stream of time- and resource-consuming ventures. The staff knows someone will get a new job, a pet program will launch, or the scope of the center will expand.

Her mind makes connections between helpers and the helpless faster than a supercomputer processes binary data. One day, she met a contractor and asked him if he would teach moms to use power tools.

"If we could get 10 moms trained as construction workers, we could find them jobs."

Lee Duckett mentioned there might be liability issues, but this didn't faze Sr. Berta.

Another day, she met a dog groomer. "Would you teach our moms to do this?"

She casts a wide net and talks up her ideas until someone gets excited enough to make them happen. It doesn't usually take long.

Sr. Berta was speaking to a United Way group in 2009 about the challenges of finding healthy protein. Mark Shaeffer, the marketing director of Bushnell Co., which sells accessories to locate deer, knew that the company's ad agency, Brothers & Co., hosted an annual charity deer hunt. Soon, 1,000 pounds of deer meat was on its way to 31st and Troost.

In the millennial year of 2000, Sr. Berta had a particularly big idea. The day before, the receptionist had announced over the intercom, "Someone left a baby at the front desk."

The staff was used to offbeat messages over the intercom. "Will the person who took Winnie the Pooh from the game room please return it? The child who donated it has changed his mind." "If anyone finds a bracelet with the word *Grandma* on it, please turn it in to Sheila Davis."

They provided the perfect soundtrack to the zany goings on at the center. Among the favorites was when Sr. Corita regularly used to announce to the entire building, "I need a man."

Hearing about a kid on a counter, though, got Sr. Berta's attention.

"What?" Sr. Berta said. "That's just nuts." She called the receptionist to confirm. The baby was in a car seat. Sr. Berta went up to get him.

RISKY BUSINESS

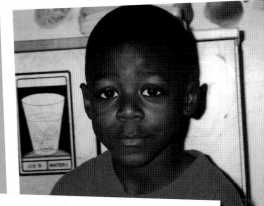

Need agitates Sr. Berta's mind to produce ideas just like sand agitates an oyster to make a pearl. She stared at the sleeping baby and couldn't stop thinking about a mother who was so desperate she would abandon her baby on a counter.

"We need to do more," she said to Sr. Corita at lunch that day. "It's not enough just to take care of the children." The idea she conceived from this would cost millions and change the focus from the end results of poverty to the root causes of it.

She began to think of offering services to the parents to help them escape the straitjacket of poverty. When Srs. Berta and Corita started the daycare, they imagined the need would be temporary. Instead, the problems facing poor families only seemed to increase. They needed to tackle bigger problems.

Sr. Berta starting talking to the board about her vision of a center that offered programs on parenting, a benefits office, therapists for children and their parents, a food pantry, and a clothes closet. The vast playground to the north of the building would be an ideal site for an addition, with a swimming pool and a gym for the neighborhood.

The center had been making do in a less-than-ideal setting. It was already crowded and had hundreds of kids on a waiting list. The half-height walls and thunderous noise weren't conducive to providing multiple services to children, much less to adults. The first rough cost estimates to realize Sr. Berta's ambitions were $32 million.

"The consensus was that the organization should expand," Kim Davis says. "But we didn't have a dime to spare."

When Sr. Berta has an idea, she is blind to any limitations. She kept talking it up. Her magnetic field soon attracted Rachael Steele, a consultant.

"You need a capital campaign," Rachael told the sisters, Kim, and Steve Callahan, the chief financial officer. "But first, you have to think about whether you really *want* to expand." She warned them that expanding would forever change the agency. The increased attention might bring in more donations, but it would also bring more scrutiny. There would be more regulations to follow and more people monitoring activities.

"Once you do this new facility, you will be forever changed," Rachael said. "You won't be a ma and pa agency anymore."

"We have made do for 29 years," Sr. Berta said. "That's long enough."

The center hired Rachael in 2000. She was shocked to find no development person on staff. There was no one even to send requests, send receipts, or make coffee. She brought more people on staff and helped the center launch a capital campaign. Money came from government and private sources.

One donor contributed some invaluable advice as well. Bill Dunn, Sr., chairman emeritus of JE Dunn Construction, convinced Sr. Berta to scale back her dreams to an $8.2 million campaign. This would allow adding 32,000 square feet of space in a new building and renovating the existing one, albeit without a pool or gymnasium.

The ground-breaking took place on September 24, 2003. The children wore hard hats and used toy shovels to mark the occasion.

DOUBLE THE FUN

In February 2006, Operation Breakthrough completed the expansion and renovation project that doubled the size of the facility and increased its licensed capacity from 353 children to more than 500. The extra space allowed the center to offer more services.

Sr. Berta asked Claudia York, who had become an emergency medical technician, to come back to the center as the health and disabilities coordinator to extend benefits to more children.

"The pay was a little better than the last time I worked for the nuns at $50 a month," Claudia says.

She couldn't believe how the center had expanded since the days she lived in the convent.

Sr. Berta and Kim stood together one afternoon admiring the renovated building and addition. Sun shone through the glass front entrance on the west and from a courtyard playground on the east. Mothers were arriving in bright-printed pants, blue jeans, or sundresses to pick up their children. They checked in at a front desk behind glass. Silver HVAC piping and industrial down lights ran between visible ceiling trusses in the light-filled space. Off-white and gray linoleum tiles spanned the space with blue and orange accent stripes.

Seventeen portraits of students lined the walls. Photographer Gloria Baker Feinstein had captured a range of expressions among their black, white, Asian, and Hispanic faces—wide-eyed, cautious, full of mirth, and a few full of sorrow. A wall of Post-It notes featured names of donors above a white picket fence.

Sr. Berta reminded Kim about the day they got the keys to the building and arrived to find water pouring through the roof.

"Those are holes in the roof," she said, pointing to the skylights. "Can you imagine we *paid* someone to put them there?"

Sr. Berta headed off to give a tour of the new facility to a church group. She took a dozen women through the five color-coded neighborhoods—green, orange, yellow, blue, and purple. Each had toys, games, and puzzles appropriate for up to 85 children ages six weeks to six years—infants, toddlers, preschoolers. This way siblings could stay together.

Classrooms once demarcated with duct tape or half-height partitions now had walls. Each neighborhood had its own social worker, education coordinator, and therapist.

Although the last elementary school classes ceased in 1986, learning was still paramount—a distinction

Issiah J.

one could easily observe. The people who worked with the children were all called teachers or teachers' aides. Children learned to say their ABCs and recognize colors before their third birthdays. Teaching moments happened in the neighborhoods and in the hallways. A group of four-year-olds marched by, chanting to the tune of "Do Wah Ditty:"

Here we come just a-walkin' down the hall
Singing do wah ditty, ditty dum, ditty doo.
Like a number one, hands by our sides and standing tall
Singing do wah ditty, ditty dum, ditty doo!
We look good, we look good!
We look fine, we look fine!
We look good, we look fine,
Here we go in our line.

Peals of laughter accompanied the melody.

The center comes close to Sr. Berta's vision. It houses a therapy center with occupational, physical, and speech therapists to help children overcome challenges. Psychiatrists at the University of Kansas see young patients by Skype on Thursdays. A state employee onsite helps parents apply for food stamps, Medicaid, and childcare. Parents can register to vote at the center. A family support section offers job counseling, GED tutoring, life-skills coaching, and parenting classes.

The center works with the Missouri Division of Family Services, Children's Mercy Hospital, five homeless shelters, two battered women's shelters, three substance abuse centers, and city programs for foster grandparents and summer youth employment.

Sr. Berta told the tour group:

Unforeseen and uncontrollable issues often surround families living in poverty. We have to be flexible and ready for just about anything—to help an evicted family find a place to sleep, console a mother who just lost a son to gun violence, give a parent whose car broke down a

Melissa Mosher with Antwain

ride to work, help a child who has been through something traumatic feel safe.

We try to provide the services that best suit each family as they move toward self-sufficiency. Our goal is always the same, but the moment-to-moment work is ever changing.

There is a birthday closet for moms to pick out gifts to give to their kids. Corita's Closet is full of children's clothing. When the teachers notice a child in the same clothes for three days, they can send them here for fresh clothes. The center gives out about 400 coats, hats, and gloves every year.

The food pantry feeds 1,000 people a month with donations from lawyers, Boy Scout troops, and other organizations.

Before the tour ends, the women are already discussing what they can do to help the Operation Breakthrough kids.

THE GRADUATES

There are now more than 8,000 alumni of Operation Breakthrough. They've become nurses, teachers, engineers, lawyers, and business executives. Not all have made wise choices. Some have committed crimes or become addicted to drugs. A few have fallen victim to the misdeeds of others. The little boy who wanted to be a fireman, "if he grew up," did not grow up. He was shot to death on his way home one day after coming to Operation Breakthrough to show off his report card.

The overwhelming majority of graduates, though, are thriving now. Here are a few:

Antwain's mother was homeless when she begged Operation Breakthrough to take her baby before "something bad happened to him" in 1999. Spending hours in a car seat had misshapen his head. He was filthy and wouldn't look anyone in the eye. One of the center's therapists, Melissa Mosher, volunteered to help "until his mother comes back." She continued to visit him after he went to live with his grandmother, until his grandmother's health declined. Then Melissa adopted him. They now live in Africa, where Antwain goes to school.

James Belton's mother, Lynne Garrett, took a job as an infant-toddler teacher at Operation Breakthrough and enrolled all of her seven children in daycare. James had behavioral issues. He ran out of classrooms shouting and punched holes in the walls. Sr. Corita wanted to kick him out. "He's too disruptive to the other students," she said.

"Let him stay," Sr. Berta pleaded. "Give him another chance."

"You said that last time…and it wasn't the first time either," Sr. Corita countered.

Lynne Garrett heard them arguing and prayed that Sr. Berta would prevail. She did. Steve Millin became his mentor. James went on to graduate from the

> *What makes the center special is how the staff becomes part of each child's family and, in some cases, becomes their families.*
>
> **—Sharon Schubert, volunteer**

> *These children belong to us. They are our responsibility. If we turn a blind eye, then we reap what happens from our neglect.*
>
> **—Chris Sill-Rogers, former board member**

> *The center really put a spark in my childhood. It kept me out of trouble and allowed me to have a lot of fun experiences.*
>
> **—DeVante Bausby, Kansas City Chiefs rookie cornerback**

Sr. Berta in costume as an angel

University of Missouri-Kansas City with a degree in mechanical engineering and now works in the field.

Stephanie Palmer-Sillimon did not become the owner of a professional baseball team as was mockingly predicted. She became a coordinator for two software companies and is now a homemaker in California who travels internationally on a regular basis.

Dwayne Ivory Bradford, the spit-baller and mischief maker, has worked for the same company for 22 years. He still keeps in touch with friends from St. Vincent's. One of them, Kevin Boggess, owns a contracting company in Iowa.

Barry Kountz earned a master's degree in environmental engineering and has worked as a project engineer in Indonesia, Iraq, Idaho, South Carolina, and Texas, where he now lives in Houston.

Kim Randolph is getting a master's degree in business administration while she works as the director of operations for P/Strada, a consulting company. She recently started her own business.

What unites them all are the mirthful memories of their days at Operation Breakthrough.

RECIPE FOR SUCCESS

"We've been blessed by such dedicated and generous people," Sr. Berta told the crowd of more than 900 at the Marriott Muehlebach Tower ballroom on April 25, 2014. Dubbed Recipe for Success, the benefit was an extravaganza with one group singing and dancing to Pharrell's "Happy," and another singing grace before the meal.

An open bar and beef tenderloin were on the menu. Rita and Lamar Hunt, Jr., were the co-chairs, and auction items included a trip to the Super Bowl in Phoenix, a VIP suite for 15 at a Justin Timberlake concert, a Florida getaway, and lunch with Kansas City Mayor Sly James. The evening raised upwards of $800,000.

It was a far cry from the first benefit at the Simpson House in about 1997. The auction items back then were potholders made by the kids.

"We thought we had really arrived," Sr. Berta says. "We ran out of food, and everybody went to Winstead's for hamburgers afterward."

Sr. Corita gazed with a wide, sparkling smile more dazzling than her sequin- and rhinestone-covered top. She was happier in the audience than on stage. She shunned the limelight. Lee Duckett recalled that St. Teresa's Academy once asked Sr. Corita to give a speech. She froze at the podium, swooned, and sat down.

Sr. Berta, who isn't fazed by crowds, quickly took over. As the one willing to take on the public speaking, she has become the public face of Operation Breakthrough. Even though neither cares a wit for credit, Sr. Berta always makes sure that Sr. Corita gets credit on a program or a plaque. Thus, their names, like their lives, have become inseparable.

The way they divided tasks fueled the organization's growth. While Sr. Corita handled the administrative tasks, Sr. Berta focused on communications, marketing, and outreach.

At every place setting were magnetized recipe cards with the picture of a child and his or her birthdate and a suggestion to bring a gift on the child's birthday. Hundreds of these magnets would go on refrigerators across the city, and a sizeable percentage would bring a gift. It's just one of many brilliant marketing ideas Sr. Berta has concocted. If she hadn't become a nun, she might be at Young & Rubicam today.

For many years, the center has laminated lucky pennies with pictures of Operation Breakthrough children for golfers at the center's annual golf tournament. The next year, at least a third of them open their wallets to show the penny they kept from the previous year.

Susie Roling with husband, Charles Menifee, at the center's Recipe for Success benefit

Sr. Berta is an artist. Her canvas is the childcare center.

—Kim Davis, former employee

The center meets all the state's standards—and then some. I would not hesitate to put my grandchild there.

—Barbara Pearl, former daycare licensing representative for the Division of Family Services

Judy Bellemere, a retired art teacher, volunteered to teach the children to paint. Some of the kids, such as Aaliyah Rayana Timmons, showed real talent. Sr. Berta liked to watch them. It wasn't long before she had the idea to turn their artwork into greeting cards, selling a package of eight for $10. The cards have brought in more than $32,000.

Sr. Berta's marketing efforts helped Operation Breakthrough expand services beyond children. These include parenting classes for residents of Amethyst Place, a home for recovering addicts with children. It runs a housing program that equips families with sofas and stoves as well as social services, and it supports a charter school. There is a full-time music therapist and a relaxation curriculum. Thirty parents attend weekly classes to become better at parenting.

The sisters marveled at the complexity of the operation that began in their convent living room.

LETTING GO OF THE REINS

Operation Breakthrough grew into an eight-million-dollar agency that served about 500 children every day and dozens of their parents. Growth also occurred in administrative duties.

"Our auditors have auditors now," Sr. Berta says. "We must follow volumes of Headstart rules and regulations. We have to record every call from parents. We are more regulated than a prison or a hospital."

As the sisters reached their 70s, the center's board of directors began to contemplate a future beyond the founders. However, evolving from an organization driven by two iconic personalities to a sustainable model has been a bumpy ride.

In 2010, the board identified succession planning as the number-one issue. Chris Sill-Rogers, the board president, appointed a succession committee made up of four prior presidents and herself.

Kids' artwork as greeting cards

Ultimately, Srs. Berta and Corita and a committee of board members and center staff recommended that Steve Callahan, Operation Breakthrough's chief financial officer, become executive director. The board voted unanimously on April 24, 2011. He had been volunteering at the center for 18 years. The announcement of his appointment said:

Steve has computerized the business, overseen the center's $13-million expansion project, suffered broken ribs while playing with children in Purple 5, filled in for both the cook and the bus driver on occasion, negotiated all the contracts, managed the upkeep of the facility, and put together the annual budgets.

When he became the executive director, the sisters took on the title of co-founders.

Steve left the position after a year. Susan Stanton stepped in as interim CEO in 2012. The former director of corrections for Jackson County had served as president and CEO of Payless Cashways and as a vice president of H&R Block. Her civic posts included serving as CEO of Kansas City Public Television and the United Way of Greater Kansas City and as vice president of the Ewing Marion Kauffman Foundation.

Susan paved the way for Sr. Corita to retire in 2013. In late 2014, Susan stepped down, and Mary Esselman took the job on January 12, 2015.

Giving up the day-to-day management of Operation Breakthrough liberated Sr. Berta to take on her greatest foe.

The rogue nuns at Sr. Corita's retirement party in 2013

Saint Luke's nursing students on Sr. Berta's bus tour

CHAPTER 17

THE FIGHT OF HER LIFE

Two dozen employees from H&R Block board the bus for one of the "City No One Sees" tours that Sr. Berta gives every few months. As the bus heads toward its first stop at Amethyst Place, Sr. Berta describes what it's like to live in poverty amid gunshots and fear:

Trauma changes your brain. The adrenaline it produces is supposed to help us deal with imminent danger—like if someone came in with a gun, we would jump under a desk. It is meant to protect you from acute danger, not to be a chronic condition. If these chemicals are always in your body, they will harm you. They can give you cancer, high blood pressure, and physical maladies.

If we can get in early, we can repair damage. We know this because we have had success. Martin Maldonado-Duran, MD, a psychiatrist, has been collecting data from Operation Breakthrough.

In 1969, the only need was childcare. All the children in our school had an address. They got a hot dinner every night. Now, almost 25 percent of our children are homeless and hungry. In the last 45 years, problems have multiplied exponentially. Utilities are a luxury in this neighborhood today. I asked an eight-year-old recently what she worried most about, and she said, "The rent." That's just nuts.

At 2732 Troost, Kim Davis, executive director at Amethyst Place, steps on the bus with a young woman and explains:

Women who have served their time and gone through drug treatment have bad histories. They've been evicted, lost jobs. These women want to do better, but no one wants to rent to them or hire them. So we started Amethyst Place. We provide a furnished apartment. Women can come here to live a sober lifestyle. They have curfews. They have to be working, in school, in drug treatment, or all of the above. We have a 60- to 65-percent recovery rate.

Several cluck approval. Kim introduces Cristina, a resident at Amethyst Place, who tells her story:

When I was a small child, the only attention I got was from adult babysitters, one of whom molested me. I got pregnant for the first time at 13. At 15, I first smoked crack with my mother. My mother introduced me to prostitution. At 17, I shot up for the first time. I had two more children. I gave my children away because I didn't want them to suffer the way I did. The more drugs I sold, the more drugs I used…alcohol, Xanax, ecstasy.

At 21, I carried guns and was arrested for crimes. I hated myself, and I hated life. I stayed in county jail for 14 months, then drug treatment. Since moving here, I have been reunited with all three of my children. I got my GED, and I will start college this fall. I just celebrated four years clean and sober. I look forward to every day.

The bus riders are quiet. As the bus heads toward its next stop, Sr. Berta continues:

The system punishes, instead of rewards, our mothers for getting ahead. There is a conspiracy to keep people down to provide a stable workforce. Our mothers are working for $8.10 an hour at McDonald's. If one gets a raise of 10 cents an hour, she loses eligibility for child-care. Fast-food restaurants have business plans that use the government to subsidize their front-line employees so they can pay executives more. The fast-food industry borders on slavery.

We've set these women up to fail because we need a cheap labor force. They've made the GED harder so our mothers can't pass it. How many of you could pass it today? There is no tomorrow for this population. If we don't give them opportunities, we will pay the price.

Near the City Union Mission at 1100 East 11th Street, a young woman named Libbie boards the bus. She tells how her life started to go downhill after her parents divorced. At the age of 14, she started smoking

pot with her mother. By 16, she had dropped out of high school and taken a job cleaning hotel rooms. She started using meth and was soon addicted.

"The drugs turned me into a monster. I stole, I lied, I manipulated," Libbie says. When her son, Logan, turned nine, she decided that if she wanted him to be a productive person, she needed to become one herself. After 33 days in a mental hospital, she applied to Amethyst, which accepted her and helped her get a job. She says:

My goal is to help you understand the underlying causes of addiction. I take full responsibility for my actions. I pay taxes; I am a hard-working community volunteer. I got a great job at Grapevine Designs.

More than half of the nation's fast-food workers use at least one form of tax-payer-subsidized assistance such as food stamps, Medicaid, or other programs.

—Diane Stafford "Tax Costs of Low Wages," *The Kansas City Star* **(4/22/14)**

Operation Breakthrough's emphasis is on getting children ready to learn

"If any of you have positions open, talk to me," Sr. Berta tells the bus passengers. As the bus heads back to the center, she concludes her tour with:

I don't think people realize how much energy it takes to be poor and how these women struggle. Do we have lazy moms? Yes. There are lazy millionaires too. Most of our parents here are either working or going to school. If they aren't, they can't come here. Our parents were born into a segregated inner city, rife with poverty, unemployment, crime, and deficient schools. Life has stacked the deck against them.

A lady called me at 3:00 p.m. and said, "I live in Independence, and there is a homeless woman with a child on my street." It took me 15 phone calls to find a place for them. If they were German shepherd puppies, it would only have taken one call.

That is nuts. Issues of poverty should be important to all economic groups in this city, state, and country. We, as a society, try to blame folks for being poor when the reality is that, for every step forward our families take, there are various regulations that force them to step back. If we wanted to, we could change this.

As a nation, we need to work together to make life better for those living in poverty. By guaranteeing the futures of these families, we are also guaranteeing the future of this country.

GENERAL SAILER ON DUTY

Giving up the administrative tasks has freed Sr. Berta to fight bigger battles. She's waging war on poverty in Kansas City. She has seen firsthand how crippling it can be. She believes the system is rigged against the 82,800 residents who live below the poverty line in Kansas City. According to the Democracy Collaborative *(community-wealth.org)*, more than 18 percent of the residents of Kansas City live in poverty—a rate greater than the rest of the state and the nation.

Sisters pose on a Harley-Davidson auctioned off at the 40th anniversary party in 2011 that raised $400,000

She knows that she will no more win this war than she will win the battle against her own mortality, but she will die trying.

She misses having her comrade at her side. Age and infirmity have done what the Catholic Church, the IRS, a gun-toting gospel preacher, and a few floods could not—separate the two.

A barricade of piled papers is still on Sr. Corita's desk, and small screens still monitor the front desk, the back door, and the playground, but she is no longer there to keep an eye on them. It's been a few months since she retired in October 2013.

Sr. Berta avoids looking at the empty office.

"The sisters used to banter back and forth," Susie Roling says. "She misses her partner."

She retrieves her smartphone from its home in her bra to call Sr. Corita. "Did you take your blood pressure medicine?"

"Don't bother me," Sr. Corita replies. Her doctors have told her that she must quit smoking. Plaque in her arteries impedes her circulation. She made a half-hearted attempt to stop.

"You are so grumpy, you need to start smoking again," Sr. Berta replies. The two sisters are no longer on an even plane. Sr. Berta has become the caretaker, dispensing unheeded health advice, and Sr. Corita resents it.

In 30 minutes, Sr. Berta calls again. "We got a lead about a building that might be for sale on 28th Street. Kim wants to expand Amethyst Place. We could go into the venture together," she tells Sr. Corita. She tries to keep her in the loop.

"Let's not call it a shelter," Sr. Corita says. "That sounds so much like a prison. I like campus so much better."

The two sisters still dream together about being able to keep Operation Breakthrough open 24 hours a day so parents could take the nightshift jobs that pay better and still have someone to watch their kids.

An hour later, Sr. Berta calls again. "You won't believe what just happened. A little boy set a fire in a wastebasket. We had to call in the fire department."

Then a woman comes into her office with a problem. Not having relatives of her own, Sr. Berta has made the Operation Breakthrough families her family. Sr. Berta responds to every problem with the urgency of a real mother. Sr. Berta calls Chris Sill-Rogers. Chris retired and told her mother once, "I will do anything to help, but I won't be a lawyer."

The sisters helped children like myself get past the pain and hurt in our lives. Even if it was only during operating hours, we had something to smile about.

—LaShantese Ward, daycare alumna

"I have a question; it isn't a legal question," says Sr. Berta. "It has nothing to do with the law."

"I know she is about to lie to me," Chris says.

"There's a woman sitting at my desk at 10:00 a.m. She has until 1:30 p.m. to decide whether to let her case go to a jury or plead guilty and get five years."

"Berta, on what planet is that not a legal question?" Chris says.

Silence.

"You don't get five years for your first rodeo," Chris says.

"She did some stupid things."

"Does she have a lawyer?"

"No, she has a public defender."

Chris refuses to represent the woman but recommends a way to negotiate with the judge.

"I see her number on caller ID, but I still pick up the phone," Chris says. "I still love her."

Sr. Berta has driven more than one employee crazy with her management style. Susie soon recognized that Sr. Berta was not the best manager. She says:

If an emergency distracted me from something she'd asked me to do, she accused me of not caring. No one is doing enough for her. Sr. Berta is always mad first. She never thinks of the positive explanation.

She believes if you aren't pissed off, then you aren't seeing the problems around you. Her expectation is that anyone who has extra should give to those who don't. She is always aware of what people aren't doing and what the human soul has the capacity to be.

Harriet Navarre, the former director of the medical clinic, says:

If I was sitting down, I wasn't busy. "Why wasn't I out more?" Sr. Berta wanted to know. When I was out, she wanted to know why she couldn't find me. She wanted me to walk the hallways and look for kids who needed attention. I was at her beck and call, yet my boss was Children's Mercy Hospital, not Sr. Berta. She would send kids for physicals without telling me, promising them I would perform them on the spot.

Chris Sill-Rogers (center), with husband Charlie Rogers (left) and Steve Millin

"If you don't have ADHD when you start here, you will when you leave," Sr. Berta tells one new hire. "And, if I didn't have it, I wouldn't have been able to get so much done."

She has done better than her lifelong companion in adapting to new ways of doing business. She's mastered her phone and can send and receive e-mails. Sr. Corita wrote everything out longhand, including budgets and work plans.

Although Sr. Berta is no longer as physically flexible, she has retained the flexibility to hold sway with diverse audiences.

At a Recipe for Success fundraiser in 2014, a politically conservative donor approached her. "You've got to teach abstinence," he said. With the impassive expression of a psychiatrist, the woman who has made birth control available to all her own children did not contradict but said noncommittally, "Young people have so many pressures."

"Yes, yes," agreed the donor. "I've got people at my company who could help you."

Sr. Berta won't let politics get in the way of help for her children.

Today, she has more resources at her disposal than when she and Sr. Corita opened their daycare with toys and bedding bought at garage sales.

Since 2011, Sr. Berta has shared her office with Christine Minkler, who works as her "handler." Christine is a calendar keeper, firefighter, and sanity preserver. Physically, she is the polar opposite of Sr. Berta. Tall and stately, she is elegantly suited and perfectly coiffed. She speaks in a throaty, feminine whisper and has a keen sense of how to keep Sr. Berta on track…and out of jail.

Jennifer Heinemann handles the bulk of publicity and media relations. Susie acts as an auxiliary mother to Sr. Berta's kids. Lee Duckett manages systems and does event planning. Together, the four women—

Christine, Jennifer, Susie, and Lee—are known as the Four Graces around Operation Breakthrough.

"It takes a village to keep her," Susie says. "She is fighting so many fires." None of them has had any success getting Sr. Berta to take care of herself.

While she has spent her life taking care of others, caring for herself is a foreign indulgence to St. Berta, like caviar or *foie gras*. She laughs off the fretting and fussing of others; their pleas for her to eat a piece of broccoli, a salad, or an apple fall on deaf ears. Instead, she calls a handful of Cheez-Its dinner.

If she is aware that her refusal to take care of herself may shorten the time she has to care for others, she shows no sign of it.

Her doctor has ordered her to use a walker, but she tries to ditch it like a prom queen might a geeky suitor. Christine reminds her to take it on a tour she is about to lead, but she rolls it out of her office and leaves it by the copying machine around the corner. She prefers to take someone's arm than be seen pushing the three-wheeled symbol of infirmity. If she uses it at all, it is to cart some toys or papers around the office.

Sr. Berta has no time for herself. She's busy launching efforts to connect rich folks with the poor. Several programs have already grown out of her The City You Never See bus tours, which she began in 2008. On one in 2012, Sr. Berta shared her dream of 100 jobs for 100 moms. Janie Gaunce, president of Grapevine Designs, answered the call to action. She hired a mom of one of the center's kids. Since then, 12 moms have gotten jobs through the effort. Kelly Wilson, the owner of Weave Gotcha Covered, relocated her business to 27th and Charlotte to make it easier for inner-city moms she's hired to get to work.

"We've got to help people who are willing to help themselves," Sr. Berta says.

Sr. Berta can fly with conservatives, liberals, atheists, and the pope. She's a chameleon.

—**Susie Roling**

Sr. Berta is trying to hold back the ocean. I can't imagine the frustration she must feel. Then, she gets up the next day and goes back to the fight.

—**Steve Millin, attorney and volunteer**

Sr. Berta doesn't have an off button. She doesn't have a way to unwind. I don't think she ever has any peace of mind.

—**Susie Roling, former employee**

> *Sr. Berta doesn't value sitting around and praying for people to get out of poverty. She values action.*
>
> **Susic Roling**

SWIM TO THE BOAT WITH STARFISH

Women from Saint Thomas More Church approach Operation Breakthrough about building a shelter, but Sr. Berta has another idea. She tells them:

Let's help women swimming toward the boat by giving them access to the same networks that you all have. If I were buying a car, I'd call someone who knew about cars. Poor women have no networks. Churches can become those networks. Would you be willing?

Women from the church agree to act as mentors for moms at Operation Breakthrough. One mom, Cherise, had earned a certified nursing assistant degree, but she couldn't find a job. Four women at the church worked in human relations at nursing homes. Within 24 hours, Cherise had a job.

The women call the program Starfish, after the story about a guy walking on the beach who returns one starfish out of hundreds to the ocean. Someone says to him, "You can't save all the starfish that way."

"I can save one," he replies.

"Once these women meet our moms, they become friends," Sr. Berta says. Sr. Berta tries to cast her net in all directions. While she works to enlist the help of middle- and upper-class Kansas Citians, she also works on legislators to make laws more favorable to the poor.

TRIP TO FANTASY RANCH

The sun is sharp as eight women gather in the center's reception area. They follow Sr. Berta to a white van bound for Jefferson City, the capital of Missouri.

Every few months, Sr. Berta likes to visit legislators to make sure those who make the laws for the poor have to shake hands with those who will either benefit or suffer from their actions.

Christine Minkler drives while Sr. Berta preps the group, which also includes a social worker, an intern, a reporter, and four moms whose kids attend Operation Breakthrough.

- Don't cut funds for early Headstart centers.
- Remove prohibition against drug felons receiving food stamps.
- Increase the budget for Medicaid.

"We've got to get down there and beat some people up," Sr. Berta says. She hands out lists of legislators to visit and key points to make. Today's points are:

The group will visit 18 senators and 31 representatives. Each will get a packet of materials that includes an Operation Breakthrough coaster. Sr. Berta tells the group:

The last time a legislator told me, "I don't want to talk to any unwed mothers. If you bring me army wives and widows, I will listen to you." Can you believe it? I told him legislators are the reason my moms don't marry. Their laws have made it an economically stupid choice.

There aren't a lot of men around because bad laws chased them away. More African-American men are in prison than were slaves in the 19th century.

To go to a shelter with a man, you have to show your marriage license. Do you carry your marriage license with you? Nobody does. But our mothers have to prove this guy is their husband. We force the men to leave, and then we say to the mothers, "Where are all the guys?"

If a mom says, "Sister, I'm getting married," I have to bite my tongue not to say, "I'm sorry." If she marries another minimum-wage earner, she loses child-care, healthcare, housing, and food stamps.

The government rewards you for failing and punishes you if you succeed. That is nuts.

Sr. Berta struggles with the fear that, by helping the poor, she may wind up hurting them instead, and it makes her perpetually angry. This prompts a discussion of other injustices.

"Why can't you use your food stamps for the salad bar at Sun Fresh?" Kelli said. "If the government wants us to eat healthy, why is there a $10 limit on spending food stamps at farmers' markets?"

Sr. Berta visiting Senator Jason Holsman's office during a trip to Jefferson City

Missouri Senator Jolie Justus and Sr. Berta at the Missouri State Capitol in Jefferson City

Topics covered range from phone chargers, to demystifying tax filing, to the proposed ban on smoking in public housing. The group is pretty fired up when they arrive at the Missouri state capitol building in Jefferson City. Designed in the Classical Revival style, the capitol features a dome that rises to an august 238 feet. Ornate columns and statuary decorate the façade.

The first stop is Chris Dunn in room 319. He's on the staff of Rob Schaaf, the District 34 representative. They discuss going "off the cliff" when someone's income rises too high to qualify for benefits. Sr. Berta tells him:

We'll pay for these kids one way or the other. We have to bring these children with us into the future, or we won't be going very far into that future. We might as well pay to make them functioning members of society today.

En route to another office, Kelli peers into the door to watch the house in session. She sees several legislators pouring over tablet computers. One is swiping through photos of women in bathing suits. A tall, suited man soon brushes her aside, saying, "I have to get in there to vote."

"What are you voting on?" Kelli asks.

"I don't know," he says. "Check the monitor."

In the van on the way home from Jefferson City, the group shares their experiences.

Sr. Berta concludes, "We've been at the fantasy ranch all day. These people don't live in reality."

The trips often wear her out, which sometimes shows in her driving. After one Jeff City trip, she was driving to visit a potential donor when she saw the flashing lights of a police car behind her.

"Was I speeding?" she asks the officer.

"No, but you were weaving and bobbing."

"Is that illegal?" she says.

"It's dangerous," the officer replies. "Have you been drinking?"

Sr. Berta sighs and shakes her head. "I'm just tired." Her expression must have convinced him of the enormity of her burden because he let her go without a ticket.

The next day, she is back in action. She calls a local school to enroll one of the recent daycare graduates. When an administrator tells her all the forms she must submit, she responds, "It's easier to get a person off death row than to get a child into your school."

Outside a child is shouting, "Leave me alone!"

"Oh," says Sr. Berta, "that sounds like Curtis." She goes to the door, and there is an eight-year-old boy trying to get away from the adult leader of his summer program group.

"I've got him," says Sr. Berta. She brings him into her office, where he throws himself on the floor. He tries to get out, but Sr. Berta stands in front of the door. She keeps talking as Curtis continues to cry. When he starts to calm down, Sr. Berta asks, "Do you want to sit over there with me?" He climbs on her lap, and she rocks him slowly. She says:

The system has really screwed him up. He came to us at three years old and was such a sweet little boy. He was in several foster homes before a family adopted him and his siblings. Then, this family gave them up, and the siblings all wound up in different foster homes.

This is a crazy society; we save tin cans and throw away children. We had a bomb threat here last fall. There is a police station a block away, but it took 30 minutes to get someone here. If there was a bomb scare at Pembroke Hill, how long do you think it would take them to get there? These kids are not valued. And it's not getting better.

Earlier in the day, she had driven to Centerville, Missouri, to bail out one of her former foster children. The police had arrested the girl for shoplifting at a Wal-Mart. A couple of Sr. Berta's children were with her in Corita's 2002 Lincoln. Ronnie was driving when a policeman pulled them over. When he asked the policeman why he stopped them, the reply was, "Driving while black."

"I don't think I would have believed it if I didn't live with black males," she says. She calls home to make sure Myles got home from work safely.

"Who will fret over them when Corita and I are gone?" she asks.

For the first time in her life, she's thinking about the future.

If there is no tomorrow, it doesn't matter what I do today. We have to give our families a tomorrow.

—Sr. Berta

Missouri Representative Rick Stream

Margie Long

HEAVENLY THOUGHTS

Margie Long comes to interview Sr. Berta. She is working on a book called *Keep Your Fork*. It will capture well-known Kansas Citians' thoughts on the afterlife.

"What is your idea of heaven?" Margie asks.

"I haven't spent a lot of time thinking about it," Sr. Berta says. "My idea of hell would be to be a gardener…and have to eat Mexican food."

"But what about heaven?" Margie presses.

"We get Headstart money, so I can't mention heaven or hell," Sr. Berta says with a smile that Margie misses as she takes notes.

"What's your view of an afterlife?" Margie tries again.

"I don't spend a lot of time thinking about it. I think more about the insanity that made this world happen," she says, gesturing to the faces of children on her walls who have lost their lives. "I used to think I knew all the answers. Now I don't even know the questions."

Then something inspires her to begin riffing like a saxophone player:

"For me, an afterlife would be a place where everyone gets along, with no economic disparity, and people can use their gifts and talents. The picture of angels sitting around with harps is stupid. Heaven seems irrelevant to me. What we ought to be doing is trying to make the earth more heavenly. This world is so far from what it should be."

"Do you believe God will reward you for your good deeds?"

"I don't know if you get rewarded for good deeds when you die. I sure don't believe that sitting in a pew will get you there or that threats of reward and punishment should be used to manipulate children."

Perhaps finally recognizing that heaven isn't on Sr. Berta's radar, Margie asks her what she considers her greatest accomplishment.

"We stayed open," she says without hesitating. "This isn't my accomplishment, though. Operation Breakthrough doesn't belong to any one or two people. The people of Greater Kansas City have built this legacy together. Their goodness has allowed this place to survive. We haven't managed to put a dent in poverty, but we have been successful at educating children," she says. "Who knows, one of our children may grow up and invent a way to wipe out poverty someday."

It is a rare moment of optimism for Sr. Berta. She's been cheered by recent calls and visits from former students, teachers, volunteers, and employees who check in regularly. She learns that Richard "Red" Chapman, the center's first cook, has spent his career in the kitchen and become a well-known chef in San Francisco. He was a banquet chef for the Mandarin Oriental Hotel there. He still volunteers regularly to cook at soup kitchens in honor of the sisters. "I still have the burn scars on my forearms from saving two hot turkeys for your Thanksgiving," he says.

At a recent plaza holiday lighting ceremony, Sr. Berta hears a woman shriek and turns to see Kim Randolph, her former student, who gives her a bear hug as tears stream down her face.

"If it weren't for St. Vincent's, I wouldn't have the life I do today," she tells her. She shows her pictures of her two children and her grandkids. "I want to help. What can I do?"

Another day, Michelle Alexander and her 16-year-old daughter drop in to thank Sr. Berta for saving their lives. Sixteen years before, Michelle entered a drug rehabilitation center and didn't have a place for her infant daughter. Sr. Berta kept the baby in her office. Michelle wants her daughter to meet the woman who gave her a chance when no one else would.

Soon after, Claudia York, the first of the flower children volunteers, comes back, as she has done almost every year, to spend time with the two women she regards as her true mothers.

Sr. Berta, whose own mother deserted her, has become a mother to so many. Wherever she goes, there is someone whose life she has graced with a love that never condemns or judges or asks for anything in return.

Parents maintain close relationships with the center

Sr. Berta (left) with Susie Roling

A NIGHTCAP

Home after a long day, she asks Sr. Corita, "Who's home? Have you taken your blood pressure medicine today? Who is picking up Vanshay? Is Ronnie going to take Tyrez to the doctor tomorrow?"

Donna Wike brings both of them their nightcap. For Sr. Corita, it is an ounce of scotch over ice. Sr. Berta's favorite drink is a Tom Collins with an ounce of gin, three ounces sweet and sour mix, and a splash of club soda, but Donna adds an extra ounce of gin, hoping it will combat the insomnia that's haunted her for decades.

Sr. Corita heads to bed around 9:00 p.m. As Sr. Berta sips her drink, the phone rings. Even though Susie Roling left Operation Breakthrough in 2014 to work down the block for Journey to a New Life, she still calls Sr. Berta every night.

"Did Vanshay and Tyrez get their report cards yet?" Susie asks.

Sr. Berta talks about Kathea, the mother of four kids who was suffering abuse from her husband. He pushed her out a second-story window. She lived in a house that didn't have gas or hot water for three years. She heated water for the kids' baths on a barbecue grill. She's doing well now.

They talk about how the center used to hide kids.

"We'd be in jail if we did today what we did then," Sr. Berta says.

"What are the plans for Kenyauta?"

"Oh, we're working on it," she says.

"What about the future?" Susie asks.

"You sound like the author that interviewed me today. I'm not very future-oriented. I just want to do what I can today."

This desire has motivated her to keep Operation Breakthrough going for 47 years, and it will get her up in the morning tomorrow.

Srs. Berta and Corita have given tomorrows to three generations of children at Operation Breakthrough

FOR THE SISTERS

Kim Randolph in the apse of St. Vincent's in Kansas City

Kim Randolph stands at the doorway of St. Vincent's school, for the first time in 45 years.

Father Jordan Fahnestock, now the principal of St. Vincent's Academy, hands her keys to the school and the church. The Society of Saint Pius X that bought the church in 1979 purchased the school about 10 years later. The Diocese of Kansas City-St. Joseph website reports, "St. Vincent de Paul: Parish closed in 1975. The church bearing this name at present is not in communion with Rome." Nor is the school that now has 200 students listed with the diocese.

Yet signs of life and learning are everywhere. Scratchy artwork hangs on a corkboard. A teacher has drawn script letters out on a chalkboard for children to emulate.

As Kim steps into the hallway, memories stop her faster than the chicken feathers she once encountered there.

"There's Sister Peggy's math class; here's where Helen Gragg taught me to type; there's where we kept the chickens; oh my goodness, here's the science room where Sr. Berta got in trouble over my fruit fly experiment," she says, like a child opening presents she never expected.

After scouring every corner of the school, including the bathroom where Sr. Corita scrubbed off her gaudy makeup, Kim heads for the church. Sun filters through the stained-glass windows, bathing the church in a celestial light. Wood, burnished to a fine sheen, makes the pews seem like they also emanate light. The SSPX congregation has patched the holes, replaced the boiler, updated the bathrooms, and refurbished the windows.

Kim walks with the reverence of a bride up the aisle where she so proudly attended Mass. She reaches a table of votive candles and puts money in a box. With the deftness of a cardinal, she lights two candles, closes her eyes, and whispers a prayer before crossing herself.

Then she steps back. As if she is uttering something too holy to say aloud, she points to the candles and whispers, "For the sisters."

Clearly, the transgressions of these two saintly sinners haven't tainted their ability to inspire faith in those around them. Despite their irreverence toward the Catholic Church and their artful dodging of conventions, commandments, and even laws, these two rogue nuns have somehow instilled a deeply religious feeling in Kim and countless others.

The religion of Sr. Berta and Sr. Corita goes beyond doctrine or dogma. Its liturgy is to pay a utility bill, buy special vitamins for an autistic child, rock an infant to sleep, and raise an abandoned child. The theology that drives them is to help, and ultimately, through doing good, they become good.

Amen.

Kim Randolph on a sentimental journey

HOW YOU CAN HELP

Volunteers are always needed at Operation Breakthrough to:

1. Rock babies or read to children.
2. Help in classrooms or in the MakerSpace.
3. Sponsor a food drive.
4. Help with the food pantry or used furniture giveaways.
5. Attend events or take a tour to learn more about the center.
6. Offer employment through a program such as Sister Berta's 100 Jobs for 100 Moms.
7. Adopt a family at Christmas or donate new toys for the Birthday Closet.
8. Donate funds so the center can continue to provide needed services for children and families.
9. Buy lots of copies of this book for your friends and family. (All proceeds support Operation Breakthrough.)

For more information, contact:

Operation Breakthrough
3039 Troost Avenue
Kansas City, MO 64109
816-329-5222
books@OperationBreakthrough.org

BIBLIOGRAPHY

Briggs, Kenneth, *Double Crossed: Uncovering the Catholic Church's Betrayal of American Nuns* (New York: Doubleday, 2006).

Budinas, Lynley, "Operation Breakthrough: A History to Learn From" (Unpublished).

Coleman, Charles M., *This Far By Faith: A Popular History of the Catholic People of West and Northwest Missouri* (Kansas City: The Diocese of Kansas City-St. Joseph, 1992).

Cowan, David, *To Sleep with the Angels: The Story of a Fire* (Ivan R. Dee, Chicago, August 1998).

Cummings, Kathleen Sprows, *New Women of the Old Faith: Gender and American Catholicism in the Progressive Era* (Chapel Hill: The University of North Carolina Press, 2010).

Fialka, John, *Sisters: Catholic Nuns and the Making of America* (New York: St. Martin's Press, 2003).

Kaylin, Lucy, *For the Love of God: Faith, Hope and the American Nun* (New York: W. Morrow, 2000).

Kelly, Kevin, *The History of the Diocese of Kansas City-St. Joseph* (Strasbourg, France: Éditions du Signe, 2003).

Reed, Cheryl L., *Unveiled: The Hidden Lives of Nuns* (New York: Berkeley Books/Penguin, 2010).

Regan, Jan, *Operation Breakthrough 40: A Loving Puzzle of So Many Pieces* (Unpublished).

Rogers, Carole Garibaldi, *Poverty, Chastity, and Change: Lives of Contemporary American Nuns* (New York: Twayne's Publishers, 1996).

Rogers, Carole G., *Habits of Change: An oral history of American nuns* (New York: Oxford University Press, 2011).

Starr, Lily, "Operation Breakthrough: A Journey of Poverty, Race and Hope" (Paper for American Civic English/History Class for Dr. Niermann/Mrs. Abernathy, 2013).

Voices of Philanthropy Magazine (Spring 2008), Interview with Sr. Berta and Sr. Corita.

ABOUT THE AUTHOR

Loring Leifer became a writer because she likes to find things—whether it's the latest medical information, a lost mitten, or a missing fact in the lives of two nuns. She's followed caddies around Winged Foot Country Club, investigated art forgeries, and tracked down railway romances—all in articles for local and national publications. A former design editor of *Interiors*, she wrote several books for Richard Saul Wurman, TED conference creator. These include *Information Anxiety*; *Follow the Yellow Brick Road: Learning to Give, Take, and Use Instructions*; and *Drugs: Prescription, Non-Prescription, and Herbal*. She also co-wrote *Younger Voices, Stronger Choices*.